THE
DARWIN
LEGEND

Also by James Moore

The Post-Darwinian Controversies: The Protestant Struggle to Come to Terms with Darwin in Great Britain and America, 1870–1900 (1979)

Beliefs in Science: An Introduction (1981)

The Future of Science and Belief: Theological Views in the Twentieth Century (1981)

(ed.) *Religion in Victorian Britain: Sources* (1988)

(ed.) *History, Humanity and Evolution: Essays for John C. Greene* (1989)

(with Adrian Desmond) *Darwin* (1991)

The
DARWIN
LEGEND

JAMES MOORE

Baker Books
A Division of Baker Book House Co
Grand Rapids, Michigan 49516

Published by Baker Books
a division of Baker Book House Company
PO Box 6287, Grand Rapids, Michigan 49516-6287

Printed in the United States of America

Library of Congress Cataloging-in-Publication Data

Moore, James R. (James Richard), 1947–
  The Darwin legend / James Moore.
     p.   cm.
  Includes bibliographical references.
  ISBN 0-8010-6321-3 (cloth)
          0-8010-6318-3 (paperback)
     1. Darwin, Charles, 1809–1882—Religion. 2. Darwin, Charles, 1809–1882—Legends. 3. Hope, Elizabeth, Lady. I. Title.
QH31.D2M59 1994
575′.0092—dc20
[B]   94–39407
                                                                        CIP

HISTORY TO BE TRUE MUST CONDESCEND TO SPEAK THE LANguage of legend; the belief of the times is part of the record of the times; and though there may occur what may baffle its more calm and searching philosophy, it must not disdain that which was the primal, almost universal motive of human life.

H. H. MILMAN, *HISTORY OF LATIN CHRISTIANITY*, 1855

IN HISTORY PERHAPS MORE THAN IN ANY OTHER DISCIPLINE ... the understanding of evidence and how to employ it is one's closest approach to that truth others seek in churches.

ROBIN WINKS, *THE HISTORIAN AS DETECTIVE*, 1969

CONTENTS

ILLUSTRATIONS

FOREWORD

AMES MOORE'S *THE DARWIN LEGEND* IS HISTORICAL DE-
tection of the absolutely best kind. Patiently, painstak-
ingly, scrupulously, exhaustively, Moore's work has
pursued the story that Charles Darwin made a deathbed
profession of the Christian faith. If repeating a story would
make it so, Darwin would be secure as a bona fide saint. But
repetition turns out to be the problem. So easy has it been
for Bible-believing Protestants (now for over a century) to
pass on this story that few have paused to ask if it is true.
Moore asks. In fact, he does not rest until he has tracked
the answer down—through the used book racks, manuscript
archives, personal libraries, and dusty newspaper deposito-
ries of three continents. What he finds—about how the story
arose, who passed it on, and what it all has to do with
Charles Darwin himself—is illuminating indeed.

What Jim Moore finds is also significant because of who
Jim Moore is. The critical matter is not pedigree, though with
degrees in science, theology, and history, Moore certainly
qualifies on that account. Nor is teaching duties exactly the
issue, though Moore has stage-managed the preparation of
several courses in the history of science at his post at Britain's
Open University. The key issue is rather expertise in Darwin
and "the Darwin industry," that tribe of academics and those
oceans of print that circle around Darwin and his nineteenth-
century work. Some years ago Moore published the finest

study yet to appear on general theological reactions to Darwin, *The Post-Darwinian Controversies* (Cambridge University Press, 1979). In 1991, with co-author Adrian Desmond, he brought out simply the best biography ever penned on the controversial nineteenth-century figure. *Darwin* (U.K. publisher, Michael Joseph/Penguin; U.S., Warner Books/Norton) is the culmination of twenty years' research. The book relates Darwin's life by a thorough, but never dull, examination of its extraordinary contexts. Quite rightly, the book has become a best-seller and has garnered prestigious awards on both sides of the Atlantic. That Moore has been willing to use Darwin's own description about himself as a "Devil's Chaplain" to make significant points about Darwin's work is enough to hint at the independence of Moore's own judgments.

To benefit fully from this book, it must be read to the end. Only after the last supporting document, the last footnote, and the last bibliographical item, does it become clear how painfully willing so many believers have been to treat the truth so casually. Only by following Moore through every last nook and cranny will the judgment of the evangelical tent-preacher, James Fegan, make sense when he calls the Darwin legend "an illustration of the recklessness with which the Protestant Controversialists seek to support any cause they are advocating."

Apart from what Moore's scintillating detective work tells us about Darwin and the ways in which legends flourish, this book also brings a sobering message about the nature of truth itself. The history of Christianity begins with one who proclaimed himself "the truth" as well as "the way and the life." In the seventeenth century, one of the most striking assertions in the remarkable book of "thoughts" *(Pensees)* by the remarkable Blaise Pascal contended that "Truth is so obscure in these times, and falsehood so established, that unless we love the truth, we cannot know it." Closer to our own day, the writings of Benjamin B. Warfield, the most sophisticated modern defender of biblical inerrancy, dwelt much on the general question of truth. Warfield, a keen amateur scientist, who wrote several learned essays on Darwin and his work, always maintained exacting standards for how believers should reason on controversial questions. "The really pressing question with regard to the doctrine of evolution," he wrote in 1895, "is not . . . whether the old faith can live with this new doctrine. . . . We may be sure that the old faith will be able not merely to live with, but to assimilate to itself all facts. . . . The only living question with regard to the doctrine of evolution still is whether it is true." By "true," furthermore, Warfield meant simply checking out what was or was not really there: whether "(1) we may deduce from the terms of the theory all the known facts, and thus, as it were, prove its truth; and (2) deduce also new facts, not hitherto known, by which it becomes predictive and the instrument of the discovery of new facts, which are sought for and observed only on the expectation roused by the theory."[1]

Surprisingly, on the question of truth Warfield, along with Pascal and Jesus himself, stood very close to Charles Darwin, the agnostic evolutionist. At the same time, as Moore shows, the historic Christian attitude toward truth could not have been more different from the attitudes adopted by many Bible-believers who also took an interest in Charles Darwin. How such a state of affairs came about is only one of the profound realities illuminated by this fascinating volume.

Mark A. Noll

ACKNOWLEDGMENTS

A THOUSAND THANKS ARE DUE TO ALL WHO HELPED ME research and write this book. I promised to credit everyone.

As the total of individuals and institutions falls well short of one thousand, I wish to thank some people many times over for extraordinary assistance: Linda S. Batty of Northfield Mount Hermon School for hospitality and a day together rummaging in the archives; the late Harriet May Bole for discussing her husband's papers; Jan and Ron Boud of Louisville, Kentucky, for cousinly hospitality and contacts; Carl C. and William Compton, *père et fils,* for helping me with Northfield research; Timothy and Libby Denny of Hingham, Norfolk, for hospitality and opening that suitcase; Paul M. Debusman of Southern Baptist Theological Seminary, Louisville, for checking the Robertson correspondence; Walter and Chrystal Bole Dutton of Des Moines, Iowa, for making the Bole papers available; the late Richard Freeman of University College London for sharing and discussing sources; Nick Furbank of the Open University for advice about family life in Abinger; Peter Gautrey of Cambridge University Library for much early guidance; Neal C. Gillespie of the University of Georgia for a kind critique; John A. Guenther of Clearbrook, British Columbia, for sharing sources and personal correspondence; Glenn K. Horridge of Cambridge, England, for information about the Sal-

vation Army; Rev. Burton K. Janes of Howley, Newfoundland, for sharing and discussing numerous sources; David
Kohn of Drew University for interest and warm encouragement; Tom McIver of the University of California, Los
Angeles, for sharing numerous sources and personal correspondence; Laurence Metzger of the University of Hawaii
for discussing his comedy about Lady Hope and Darwin's
deathbed; Rev. William Moreland of Orillia, Ontario, for
information about Ivan Panin; the Mutch family diaspora
for responding to my queries about John Mutch; Mark Noll
of Wheaton College for hosting and interceding as usual;
Ron Numbers of the University of Wisconsin for biblio-
graphic tips and expert advice on "seventh-day" history;
David Oldroyd of the University of New South Wales for
sharing sources and photographing Lady Hope's grave;
Robert D. Posegate of Northwestern College for helping me
find the Bole papers; Craig J. Pringle of Webster City, Iowa,
for sharing numerous sources; the late Rev. George R.
Probert, my grandfather, for sending evangelical ephemera;
Chris Royer and his mother Maria for interviews and hospitality; Colin Russell of the Open University for both introducing me to the Darwin legend and sharing sources and
personal correspondence; Anne Secord of the Darwin correspondence project, Cambridge University Library, for supplying letters and microdarwiniana; Susan Sheldon for re-
searching Lady Hope's last days in Sydney; and Jim Wallis
for hospitality to a fellow sojourner.

For answering peremptory notes, rushing photocopies
and illustrations, and generally letting me pester them, I wish
to thank: Paul E. Almquist of Eastern Baptist Theological
Seminary; Dick Aulie; Laura C. Bailey of the Iowa State University Alumni Association; the late F. F. Bruce of the University of Manchester; William Bynum of the Wellcome Institute for the History of Medicine, London; A. J. Cain of
the University of Liverpool; Vern Carner; Edward A. Coray
of Wheaton College; Mrs. D. Corbett; Bolton Davidheiser

of Westmont College; Enock C. Dyrness; Alfred Eggaford; Paul Fayter of the University of Toronto; Gordon E. Fish of the University of Illinois; Harold A. Fiess of Wheaton College; Herbert A. Fryling of the Sunday School Times Foundation; Jack Haas of Gordon College; Roger Hahn of the University of California at Berkeley; Clarence B. Hale; Joy Harvey of the Darwin correspondence project, Cambridge University Library; Walt Hearn; Robert E. Kofahl of the Creation-Science Research Center; Eric Korn; Amy McGrath; Russell L. Mixter of Wheaton College; John Mostert of the American Association of Bible Colleges; Alvin F. Oickle of the *Greenfield Recorder*, Greenfield, Massachusetts; Stephen W. Paine; William J. Peterson of *Eternity* magazine; A. Radcliffe-Smith of the Evolution Protest Movement; Robert Ratcliffe; Delbert R. Rose of Wesley Biblical Center; David Rosevear of the Creation Science Movement; Wilbert H. Rusch Sr. of the Creation Research Society; the late Ernest R. Sandeen of Macalester College; Emma Moody Smith; Malcolm Taylor; W. Lloyd Taylor of Mount Vernon Nazarene College; Nicolas Walter of the Rationalist Press Association; Timothy P. Weber of Conservative Baptist Theological Seminary; and Anson Yeager of the *Argus-Leader*, Sioux Falls, South Dakota.

Librarians worked wonders, conjuring arcana on demand. For providing me facilities, in person or by post, I am grateful to the reference and archival staff at the following educational bodies: Andover Newton Theological School (Diana Yount); Andrews University (Louise Dederen); Biola College and Talbot Theological Seminary; Cambridge University (Godfrey Waller); Canadian Theological Seminary (Ron Baker); Covenant Theological Seminary (Joseph Hall); Hampden-Sydney College (Catherine Pollari); Harvard Divinity School (Laura Whitney); Illinois Institute of Technology; Imperial College of Science and Technology, London (Anne Barrett); Keele University (Martin Phillips); Knox College, University of Toronto; Moody Bible Institute; Northern Baptist Theological Seminary; Northfield Mount Hermon School; Oberlin College Library (Emily M. Belcher, Ray English); Open University (Tony Coulson); Salem College, Salem, West Virginia (Dennie Pickens); Southern Baptist Theological Seminary, Louisville; Taylor University (David C. Dickey); University of Massachusetts at Amhurst (Virginia Garraud); University of London, Senate House; Vennard College (Patricia Bowen, Alice Collins); Virginia Historical Society (Janet B. Schwarz); Washington and Lee University (Erin Foley); Westminster Theological Seminary, Philadelphia (Grace Mullen); and Wheaton College (Roger Phillips).

Other research centers opened their doors and mailboxes to myriad odd requests. I wish to thank the following institutions and individuals: American Baptist Historical Society (William H. Brackney); American Philosophical Society, Philadelphia (William Montgomery); Anglican Cemetery Necropolis, Sydney, New South Wales; Archives of Ontario, Toronto (Leon Warmski); Billy Graham Center Library and Archives, Wheaton, Illinois; Bishopsgate Institute, London (David Webb); Boston Public Library; British Library; British Newspaper Library, Colindale; Bromley Central Library, Bromley, Kent; Chalmers Presbyterian Church, Toronto (Wilfrid Cooke); Clarksburg-Harrison Public Library, Clarksburg, West Virginia (Frank A. Langer); Corporation of Hamilton Public Library (Katharine Greenfield); Darwin Museum, Downe, Kent (Philip Titheradge, Solene Morris); L'Eglise Presbyterienne au Canada (John S. Moir, Donald C. MacDonald); Ellen G. White Estate, Washington, D.C. (Ron Graybill); Ellen G. White/SDA Research Centre, Avondale College, Cooranbong, Australia; Evangelical Library, London; Frances E. Willard Memorial Library for Alcohol Research, Evanston, Illinois; General Register Office, London; High Court of Justice in Bankruptcy, London; Kent Archives Office, Maidstone; Library of Congress, Washington, D.C. (Paul T. Heffron); Metropolitan Toronto Central Library (Edith G. Firth); Moody Museum, East Northfield, Massachusetts; National Library of Canada, Ottawa (Don Carter); National Meterological Archives, Bracknell, Berkshire (M. J. Wood); New York Public Library; Presbyterian Historical Society, Philadelphia (Mary Plummer); Principal Register of Probate, London; Public Record Office, Kew; Registrar-General, Hobart, Tasmania; Registry of Births, Deaths and Marriages, Sydney, New South Wales; Salvation Army Archives and Research Center, New York City; Salvation Army International Heritage Center, London (Cyril J. Barnes); Scottish Record Office, Edinburgh (A. Mackerracher); Sioux Falls Public Library, Sioux Falls, South Dakota (Lorraine Stapleton); Springfield City Library, Springfield, Massachusetts (Ellen M. Coty); State Library of New South Wales, Sydney (Baiba Irving); Wedgwood Museum, Barlaston, Staffordshire (Gaye Blake Roberts); and YMCA Historical Library, New York City (Ellen Sowchek).

For permission to study, and in instances quote from, manuscripts and other unpublished material, I am grateful to: Billy Graham Center Library and Archives, Wheaton, Illinois; Bishopsgate Institute, London, for the Bradlaugh Papers; British Museum (Natural History) and Royal College of Surgeons for the Darwin papers in the Darwin Museum, Downe, Kent; Chalmers Presbyterian Church, Toronto, for the Church Archives; George Pember Darwin and the Syndics of Cambridge University Library for the Darwin Archive; Timothy Denny of Hingham, Norfolk for the Denny Family Papers; Imperial College Archives, London, for the Huxley Papers; Keele University Library and The Trustees of the Wedgwood Museum, Barlaston, Staffordshire, for the Wedgwood-Mosley Collection; Library of Congress for the William Jennings Bryan Correspondence; Moody Museum, East Northfield, Massachusetts, for the Moody Papers; National Meterological Archives, Bracknell, Berkshire; Nebraska State Historical Society, Lincoln, and the Bole family for the S. James Bole Papers; Northfield Mount Hermon School, East Northfield, Massachusetts, for the School Archives; Salvation Army Archives and Research Center, New York City; Southern Baptist Theological Seminary, Louisville, for the A. T. Robertson Correspondence; and YMCA Historical Library, New York City.

My first ideas for this book were aired before diverse academic groups. For stimulating feedback I am grateful to the organizers and the audiences in the Thames Polytechnic Open Lecture Series, November 1979; the Open University History of Science Seminar, March 1980; the American Society of Church History annual meeting, December 1980; and the Biology Group Seminar at Darwin College, Cambridge, June 1981. For incentive to put my work in final form I wish to thank the Institute for Research in the Humanities at the University of Wisconsin, Madison, which invited me to deliver the substance of this book as the 1994 William Coleman Memorial Lecture.

Funding for my research was provided by the Open University through the Overseas Travel Subcommittee and the Arts Faculty Research Committee.

Finally, those I cannot thank enough, or don't know how to: Ralph Colp Jr. for constant generosity and warm advice; Suzan Davies for continuing friendship; Adrian Desmond for inspiration and editing; John and Ellen Greene for moral support; Sam Haley for battling the blues; Chris and Barrie Vincent at the White Hart for endless cheers; Alison Winter for wisdom and encouragement; Ruth Moore, Gordon, Pat, and Tom for being family; and above all Jessica Drader, my very own. This book is for her.

J. M.
CAMBRIDGE, ENGLAND
ST. VALENTINE'S DAY, 1994

GHOSTS, COFFINS, AND LADIES

D
ID YOU KNOW THAT CHARLES DARWIN BECAME A *Christian before he died? It's true. I read about it once in a book—or was it a magazine? I forget. Any way, my father told me about it first, when I was studying biology in school. He said that Darwin gave up his theory of evolution on his deathbed and put his faith in the Bible. No, I can't remember where Dad learned about it. I think he said it was in a tract he picked up at church. But I've asked other folks and they know about Darwin's conversion, too. They say that a lady heard it from his own mouth. Her name was 'Hope,' I think. Isn't it wonderful? Darwin spent his whole life fighting against creation, then at the last moment he read the Bible and believed. What a testimony to the power of God's Word!"*

So I have heard countless times from wide-eyed believers. Their reports are routine. Whenever I lecture or broadcast about Darwin in North America I am inevitably asked about his "deathbed conversion." Some inquirers are perplexed, others persuaded, but all devoutly hope that as a historian I can prove the story true.

My first reaction was total disbelief. I had studied Darwin's religion for years. I knew his deathbed well: Darwin died as he had lived, an agnostic. The conversion story was an obvious myth, just like so many deathbed tales—manufactured, malicious.

21

For centuries religious busybodies have not only prayed for, but preyed upon famous freethinkers. Spinoza, Voltaire, Tom Paine, Pierre Laplace, Emma Martin, Emile Littré, Thomas Huxley, Luther Burbank, and Bertrand Russell were all rumored to have seen the light before they died. Lesser reprobates suffered worse indignities. Clergymen would break into their death chambers, struggling past the family to the bedside in hopes of extracting a repentance. This unholy meddling made godless dying an ordeal. Burly unbelievers were summoned to keep vigil at deathbeds, while scribes stood by, pens poised, to take down profane last words. These heroic scenes were then recounted in cheap tracts to ward off the religious vultures—titles like *Infidel Death-beds* and *Death's Test; or, Christian Lies about Dying Infidels*. The Darwin deathbed story was, I felt sure, just one more dastardly fib.[1]

Then I *read* the story for the first time—not one of the versions endlessly recycled in tracts, but the story as originally published in 1915. To my amazement, it was a firsthand account by "Lady Hope." The noble lady did not report a death scene or a conversion, but merely a strange interview she had had with Darwin some months before he died. And fanciful as her story was, I saw at once that parts of it might be authentic.[2] This threw me completely. Perhaps all along I had been dismissing a legend, not a myth.

Myths grow up around famous (or infamous) historical figures because they seem to stand apart from other mortals, out of time. Their lives acquire a numinous aura, their deaths an ominous aspect, and weird tales about them circulate. One authentic Darwin myth is the local tradition that he "still lives and visits his old home. . . . His aged and ghostly figure may still be observed" pacing the grounds. Darwin's shade is even said to be one of seven haunting the house across the road.[3] Stories like this have a history, but their origins are the province of folklorists and social psychologists, not professional historians.

Legends by contrast are about real events. Though unreliable, they have a factual basis that historians can explore. The legend of "Darwin's wandering coffin" is a good example. For years it was rumored that a coffin made for Darwin had been kept at a house in his village, then put on display in a nearby pub, and finally used to inter its maker, John Lewis. In fact, a carpenter named John Lewis had built a rough oak coffin within hours of Darwin's death on April 19, 1882. It was returned to him when a resplendent one was supplied for Darwin's state funeral in Westminster Abbey. But the later movements of Lewis's coffin are uncertain, known only by hearsay and conjecture. The dusty old box has never been traced. Nor indeed has a record been found of Lewis's own death and burial.[4] The whole story must be taken with a substantial pinch of salt, though it is rooted in local history.

Is the Darwin deathbed story a similar legend—a grotesque gloss on real historical events? I now believe so. But I reached this conclusion only by the most awkward, circuitous route. It took many years and miles of shoe leather to come up with the right evidence. Only the first step was straightforward: tracking down "Lady Hope."

No one I asked, neither believers in the legend nor skeptics, could tell me anything about her. In tracts she was usually identified as "Lady Hope of Northfield, England." But what about the "Lade Hope" I came across, or the "Lady Pope"? According to one source, her real name was "Lady Ogle." She had worked with the Plymouth Brethren in England and claimed to have seen Darwin "on numerous occasions in the mission where she . . . attended." Once she had even "seen him weep" during a service. Or perhaps, as some suggested, the lady who started the deathbed story was simply Darwin's devout and well-meaning wife, using the likely name of "Hope."[5]

In consternation I went back to the "Lady Hope" who reported meeting Darwin. Was a woman of that name known at the time of his death? If so, what was her occupation? Did she live until 1915, when the Darwin story was published? I fired off letters, plundered my local library, and ransacked London archives. Within a few weeks I had brought the lady vividly to life.

She was born Elizabeth Reid Cotton on December 9, 1842, in the parish of Longford, near Launceston, Tasmania, the eldest child of Captain (later Sir) Arthur Cotton of the Royal Engineers and Elizabeth Learmouth, from a local landowning family. Young Elizabeth married twice—in 1877 to Admiral Sir James Hope (who died in 1881), and in 1893 to the philanthropist T. Anthony Denny (who died in 1909). She bore no children but was a prolific author, leaving some thirty titles under her nom de plume, Lady Hope, in the British Library Catalogue. These publications dealt with evangelistic and temperance themes; many contained personal anecdotes reminiscent of the Darwin story. Lady Hope emigrated to the United States in 1913 and eventually settled in California. She sailed for England a few years later but died en route, on March 8, 1922, at Burilda Private Hospital in Summer Hill, a suburb of Sydney, Australia. Her burial took place in the Church of England cemetery at Rookwood.[6]

This tantalizing information prompted a torrent of questions. What sort of person was Elizabeth Cotton, alias Lady Hope? Who were her friends? How did she spend her time? What was she doing in the period when she claimed to have visited Darwin? Can her account of their meeting be trusted? Is any of it credible? Why did she wait over thirty years before telling her story? Or did she? And what happened after its publication? Did she repeat herself, or recant? How did the Christian public react?

I posed similar, searching questions about Darwin. How did his religious faith develop? When did he reject Christianity, and why? Was he likely to have changed his beliefs in later years? What was his spiritual state in the last months

of his life? Did he receive visitors at that time? Was his wife
also present? How did she and the family handle religious
issues? Would they have opened the door to Lady Hope?
What did the Darwin children and grandchildren make of
her published story?

All these questions I tackled in the spirit of Darwin himself, who was once called "the greatest criminal detective
the world has yet seen." Of course the creation of the world
cannot be regarded as a crime, yet Darwin unravelled its se-
crets by snooping, prying and poking around, teasing out
the evidence for evolution. He found no eye-witness, no
smoking gun. His evidence was circumstantial, cumulative,
and finally convincing. Men have been sentenced to death,
or reprieved, on the strength of such evidence.[7] And I was
prepared to go to the wall—or rather, send the legend there—
for the circumstantial evidence of Lady Hope's story.

This book reports my findings over the past twenty years.
It may be revised by further research, but at least it exposes
the deathbed legend once and for all. My sleuthing has taken
me to three continents; through acres of decaying newsprint
and reams of domestic correspondence; over mountains of
monographs and even on a wild goose chase into the Alleghenies in search of Darwin's penitent "other book." I have
located over one hundred occurrences of the legend in manuscript and print, including eleven original sources, at least
two of which may be unconnected with Lady Hope. I have
also compiled the Darwin family's angry reaction to the conversion story in ten private and published letters. All this evidence is transcribed or fully documented in the appendixes.

The Darwins were not alone in opposing the deathbed legend. Freethinkers and other evolutionists have debunked it
repeatedly. But they still find Lady Hope to be a "shadowy
figure" and a "mystery." So also, ironically, do evangelicals.
In recent years some of them have jumped on the evolutionists' bandwagon. Anxious that their belief in creation should
appear "scientific," they have rushed to distance themselves

from the legend. The story attributed to Lady Hope is "completely false" and has "no basis in fact," they say. Lady Hope's existence is irrelevant.[8]

None of these parties has got it right—not the neo-creationists, not the evolutionists, not even the Darwins. Lady Hope was a real person; the story she told has some historical merit, though it immediately launched a legend. Now, for the first time, her story can be traced to a precise period in Darwin's life, and its significance for understanding his posthumous reputation can be assessed. There may be crumbs of comfort for all concerned in what follows, but there are also faults to be found on every side. The historical Darwin is no one's monopoly.

My account begins with a narrative of Darwin's religious development, from prospective parson to closet agnostic (chaps. 1–2). It was a tortuous passage: as an evolutionist Darwin feared for his respectability, while his wife Emma feared for his eternal salvation. The tensions he experienced—most evident in his famous illness—were recreated after his death when the family quarreled bitterly over publishing the religious part of his private autobiography (chap. 3). A compromise was struck to protect Emma, requiring that the most personal and pointed passages be suppressed. In the family's *Life and Letters* the world was given a moderate, respectable, agnostic "Darwin" long before Lady Hope spoke out.

Lady Hope's status as a national temperance campaigner was at a peak in the period when she allegedly met Darwin. And there are good reasons for placing her in or around his village at the time she claimed to have visited him (chap. 4). She first published her account of their interview in the United States, doubtless because it was opportune. The story, though imaginative, cannot be dismissed as pure invention. It contains striking elements of authenticity, to which Lady Hope privately added convincing new detail (chap. 5). The religious press picked it up and it spread like wildfire, provoking heated protests by the Darwins, who referred inquirers to the *Life and Letters* (chap. 6). Their promotion of the official "Darwin" was just as opportune as Lady Hope's promotion of hers. In 1929, through the family's good offices, the Darwin home was presented to the nation as a shrine to respectable, evolutionary agnosticism.

The uncensored text of Darwin's autobiography finally appeared in 1958, showing his definitive rejection of Christianity. Two years later the deathbed legend was first tentatively exposed by a sympathetic unbeliever. Evangelicals have scarcely noticed. The old, stale slur on Darwin still circulates, even on television.[9] "The children of this world are in their generation wiser than the children of light."

I

A MAN IN CONFLICT

IRONY AND AMBIGUITY SHROUDED THE LIFE OF CHARLES Darwin. He moved uneasily through the world, a perambulating paradox. Friend of the clergy and godsend to radicals, a respectable gent with a revolutionary idea, he felt as if he were a "Devil's Chaplain."[1]

He was born of middle-class Nonconformity in the West Midlands of Regency England. His Whig grandfathers abetted the region's growing industrialism, Erasmus Darwin through rhapsodical poetry, Josiah Wedgwood I by retailing pottery. Josiah was a conservative Unitarian, Erasmus a freethinker and wealthy physician. His son Robert took after him in both ways. Robert established a large and lucrative practice in the market town of Shrewsbury and there groomed the grandsons, Erasmus (b. 1804) and Charles (b. 1809), to follow the family tradition in medicine. In the 1820s he sent them to his alma mater, Edinburgh University. Erasmus eventually qualified as a physician but was himself unwell. Dr. Darwin pensioned him off at the age of twenty-five and "Ras" became a dyspeptic dilettante in London.

Charles was a keener disappointment. At Edinburgh his studies suffered after he struck up a friendship with Britain's top invertebrate zoologist, Dr. Robert Grant. A sponge specialist, Grant became Charles' walking companion and extramural tutor. Together they scoured the Firth of Forth for exotic sea-life and attended the university's Plinian Society,

where students and staff debated hot topics in natural history.
Grant was an evolutionist, following the French *philosophe*
Lamarck; the Plinian served as platform for his and other
members' radical, materialist ideas. On March 27, 1827,
Charles was present to communicate a discovery about ma-
rine organisms. Grant enlarged on the finding; then the meeting erupted when one of the presidents, a fiery unbeliever, read
a paper arguing that mind and consciousness are not spiritual properties, but only by-products of the brain's activity.
This was Grant's view, as Charles knew, and evidently a perilous one. The paper was struck from the minutes.

A few weeks later Charles dropped out of medicine and
returned home. To cure his indirection Dr. Darwin prescribed
a stint at Cambridge University to train for the Church of
England. Charles had been baptized an Anglican, steeped in
his mother's Unitarianism, and schooled at Shrewsbury under
a future bishop. A Church career would suit him. The doctor, a shrewd pragmatist, saw it as a safety net for second
sons. Charles himself viewed the prospect with the reasoned
reserve typical of ordinands at the time. A country parish
would make few demands on his faith; he would have a respectable station, a guaranteed income, and above all the
leisure to indulge his Edinburgh interest in natural history.

In 1828 Charles went up to Christ's College to study for
the B.A. and ordination. Here his tutors were untainted by
French radicalism—clergymen like the botany professor
John Henslow and the geology professor Adam Sedgwick,
who taught that species and society alike were kept stable
by God's will. This was the reigning orthodoxy in Cambridge; everyone respected it more or less. Unbelievers were
unwelcome, as Charles soon learned.

It happened the second spring, while he was enjoying himself as usual, drinking, gambling, and collecting beetles: the
veteran radicals Robert Taylor and Richard Carlile tramped
into town. They were infamous freethinkers with prison
records for blasphemy and sedition. Worse, Taylor had

trained at Cambridge for the Church and was still in holy orders. He was a turncoat priest conducting an "infidel home missionary tour," assailing the faith "by law established." With Carlile he issued a challenge to the chief divines and the college heads to debate the historical existence of Jesus. The printed circular was also distributed to students and a copy written in Latin and Greek was pinned to the university library door.

The infidels were courting persecution. It began when a messenger from the vice-chancellor demanded that the landlord in whose house they were staying hand over his lodging-house license. When he refused, a bill was posted in all the colleges stating that the license had been revoked—the house was now off-bounds. The man was ruined, though no offense against university regulations had been committed. He appealed in vain to the vice-chancellor, as did Taylor and Carlile. Meanwhile a gang of vigilantes prepared to avenge the hapless landlord by ducking the radicals in the river. When Taylor and Carlile got wind of the plan they quickly slipped out of town—not wholly empty-handed. They had uncovered about fifty young collegians prepared to avow "Infidelity."

Charles was not among them; his beliefs remained conventional. But in the close-knit collegiate community the moral mayhem could hardly have escaped his notice. Certainly by 1831, when he took his degree, Taylor's example as a renegade divine was familiar from chats with his brother in London. Ras was the most radical Darwin since his grandfather: an anti-Church freethinker addicted to Whig democracy and German philosophy. He was political, with an eye on the streets and an ear for gossip as the Whig reforms of the 1830s passed into law. In the capital he was Charles' chief informant when Taylor again fell foul of the religious establishment.

Taylor now had a pulpit in "The Rotunda," a ramshackle building flying a French *tricolore* flag—London's center of republican atheism. Here on weekdays activists plotted the downfall of rich, port-sipping priests and the return of po-

litical power to the people. On Sundays Taylor provided
light entertainment: he donned rakish robes and preached
bombastic "sermons" before packed artisan audiences. In
one of these parodies Taylor pronounced "God and the
Devil . . . to be but one and the self-same being." For this
he was dubbed "the Devil's Chaplain" and his sermons circulated by the thousand in a disreputable rag, *The Devil's
Pulpit*. In spring 1831 a clerical spy ring, the Vice Society,
reported him to the authorities. He was arrested, convicted
on seven counts of blasphemy, fined heavily, and on July 4—
Independence Day in the United States, sympathizers
noted—sentenced to two years' imprisonment. The papers
were full of the story. *The Times* even editorialized on Taylor's plight and printed a letter from him exposing the cru-
elties he suffered in Horsemonger Lane jail.[2]

By late summer the case had jogged freethinkers across the
country—and their devout brothers. Charles never forgot the
Devil's Chaplain, even if for now the example of an apostate
priest held little interest for him. He was relishing his freedom. In August he took a geological field trip in north Wales
with Professor Sedgwick. Back in Shrewsbury he was set to
shoot partridges when he found a letter from Professor
Henslow with an offer of a place as captain's companion on
H.M.S. *Beagle*. This was the turning-point of his life. His
path to a country parish was now diverted via a voyage
around the world.[3]

Five years abroad, collecting and speculating, sheltered
Charles from the political sea-change at home. Of course
the evangelical Captain FitzRoy was a constant reminder of
Tory-Anglican prejudice, and slave-owning colonial
Catholics outraged Charles' abolitionist morals. But nothing more, save letters and the odd newspaper, prepared him
for the return to London. The ferment was palpable in
March 1837 when he moved in near Ras to seek expert help
with his *Beagle* collections. Successive Whig governments
had tackled corruption, extended the franchise, and opened

up public offices to non-Anglicans. Angry radicals, unap-
peased, demanded further concessions—press freedom, universal suffrage, the disestablishment of the Church. A national movement was already under way: by May 1838
thousands were marching for electoral reform, leading to a
general strike in August 1842. For Britain these were the
century's most revolutionary years; for Charles they were
the most formative.

He entered scientific society, his fame as the *Beagle*'s naturalist preceding him. Here materialism and evolution were
debated as in Edinburgh, though again he had little to pre-
pare him—only his shipboard copy of Charles Lyell's *Principles of Geology*, with its lofty refutation of Lamarck. Evolution had been taken up by radical naturalists and medical
men, not just as a true theory of life, but as an ideological
weapon. They used it to thrash the corrupt, miracle-mon-
gering creationists—Oxbridge dons, Tory politicians,
wealthy placemen—who kept scientific institutions in a
stranglehold, curbing access to patronage and entry to the
professions. To the radicals, evolution meant material atoms
moving themselves to ever higher states of organization, just
like social atoms—humans—could. It was the natural le-
gitimation of democracy, in science and society alike.[4]

One of the radicals was Charles' Edinburgh friend Dr.
Grant, now professor of zoology in London's new, non-An-
glican University College—the "godless" college in Gower
Street. He was the capital's leading Lamarckian, and notorious. His efforts to transform the aristocratic Zoological
Society had collapsed after he crossed swords with his rival,
the Anglican anatomist Richard Owen. Grant was ousted
from the governing council and left the Society, losing support for his research. The affair damaged his career ir-
reparably and left bitter feelings, as Charles noticed when
he showed up for a meeting.[5] It was all so salutary. He now
avoided his old tutor, even though Grant offered to exam-
ine his coral specimens from the *Beagle*.

Charles was on the make. Within months he had a huge government grant by courtesy of his Cambridge patrons to publish his *Beagle* research; he recruited Owen to the project to describe the fossil mammals. Lyell himself was Charles' patron at the elite Geological Society and saw him on to the governing council. Here Charles read long papers before the Oxbridge savants; the president Rev. William Whewell asked him to become a secretary. All in all, the young gent looked like paragon of respectability.[6]

And so he was, in public. Privately, in the year Victoria acceded to the throne, he turned traitor. The voyage, the political ferment, and specialist reports on his collections had shattered his orthodoxy: he became a closet evolutionist. In a series of pocket notebooks, known only to himself and Ras, he began working out a theory that would displace Grant's godless Lamarckism and revolutionize the study of life. His aim was to explain the origin of all plant and animal species, including the human mind and society, by divinely ordained natural laws. Such a theory was metaphysically dangerous—"oh you Materialist!" Charles jotted half in jest—and it was sure to be damned as atheistic by those he least wished to offend. So secrecy was vital.[7] Radicals had jeopardized their careers, even their freedom, for lack of discretion. Charles was no radical.

Of course his theory would not have shocked Ras's freethinking friends among the urban gentry. They met for intellectual dinner parties, with Charles as a guest. Ras was probably the only evolutionist, but Harriet Martineau, a Whig apologist and liberal Unitarian, accepted materialism as a Christian truth. Thomas Carlyle, the reforming historian, shared her conviction that the universe obeys Eternal Law. And the Darwins' cousin Hensleigh Wedgwood, though an immaterialist, believed in the natural development of language.[8]

Such moral support was welcome but it hardly calmed Charles' fears. He was often unwell, with headaches and stomach troubles. Insomnia and nightmares plagued him, and once he even dreamt of public execution. He felt like a "prisoner" in London, hemmed in by "dirty odious" streets, tied down by his *Beagle* work, theorizing on evolution and dreading the consequences.[9] His future as a naturalist was at stake, his reputation, his respectability. A word out of turn and he would be ruined.

In his notebooks he devised protective strategies, lest he should ever publish. He would dissociate his theory from Lamarck's tawdry *transformisme* and express himself in safe, nonmaterialistic language. He would show how his theory, like all true science, promoted progress, no matter what critics might say. "Mention persecution of early Astronomers," he scrawled, those like himself who pushed "their science a few years in advance only of their age."[10]

Above all, he would package the theory for Anglican creationists, pointing up its superior theology. Surely a world populated and progressing by natural law was "far grander" than one in which the Creator interferes with himself, "warring against those very laws he established in all organic nature." Just think—Almighty God miraculously making allied species on adjacent islands, like "the Rhinoceros of Java & Sumatra," or lavishing on earth the "long succession of vile Molluscous animals" since Silurian times! "How beneath the dignity of him, who is supposed to have said let there be light & there was light."

"Bad taste," Charles added as an afterthought. He worried that his theological one-upsmanship might offend. But in mid-1842 he took up the theme again in a pencil sketch of his theory, which he now called "natural selection." It seemed so obvious: nature "selects" the best adapted through a struggle for existence, producing organisms of "the most exquisite workmanship." The laws causing "death, famine, rapine, and the concealed war of nature" bring about "the highest good, which we can conceive, the creation of the higher animals." Good from evil, progress from pain—this was a boost for God. "The existence of such laws should exalt our notion of the power of the omniscient Creator."[11]

Charles might have sounded like a parson but the Church was the last thing on his mind. Geology had become his first love, publishing the *Beagle* research his first priority. Also his religious beliefs had changed. He knew that his theory undermined the "whole fabric" of Anglican orthodoxy. Let one species alter, he noted brashly, and the whole creationist edifice "totters & falls."[12] With such ideas he was plainly unfit to take holy orders, never mind geology or his bad health. He was living on the brink of the abyss, which had cost others dear. What he needed now was a low-profile livelihood and a safe place to work.

In 1838 Dr. Darwin, heartened by his ambition, had opened the family purse to endow him as a gentleman naturalist. Months later, Charles married his first cousin Emma Wedgwood, celebrated his thirtieth birthday, and made plans to escape from London. In September 1842 the Darwins moved to the Kentish village of Downe, sixteen miles from the metropolis. It was the ideal habitat for a nervous evolutionist: a small rural community at the "extreme verge of [the] world." Among the rustics Charles would keep society at bay while fulfilling his old ambition to be a parish naturalist. Appropriately, his new home was the former parsonage, Down House. It stood a quarter-mile south of the church, backed by fifteen acres of pasture. Here his clerical camouflage was complete.[13]

At Downe Emma became his full-time nurse and the mother of ten. She was a sincere Christian like all Wedgwoods of her generation: Unitarian by conviction, Anglican in practice. Charles differed with her, painfully.

It was partly his own fault. Dr. Darwin had warned him that a husband should conceal his religious doubts lest the wife fear for his eternal salvation. Charles had ignored the advice, revealing all to Emma while courting. She was one of the first to hear about his theory after Ras and the doctor. The news caused her "melancholy thoughts." She poured out her heart in a letter, pleading with him to read her favorite scripture, "our Saviours [sic] farewell discourse" in the Gospel of John, where Jesus warns: "If a man abide not in me, he is cast forth as a branch and is withered; and men gather them, and cast them into the fire, and they are burned." Again, when she first became pregnant, Emma wrote in distress, for "when I talk to you . . . I cannot say exactly what I wish." What if she died in childbirth? Would her "dear Charley" join her in heaven? She knew that the wretched example set by Ras, who had "gone before you," had removed some of the "dread & fear" that accompanies doubt, but for her it would be a nightmare, she finished, "if I thought we did not belong to each other forever."[14]

Yet Charles only doubted; he had not renounced the faith. There was hope for him. Emma's anxiety remained a sad undercurrent in the marriage, her heartache and prayers increasing with his illness. The symptoms became kaleidoscopic—vomiting, shivering, dizziness, flatulence. He suffered for hours each day and often could not work. Doctors found nothing wrong, nor could Emma.[15] His problem lay beyond medicine. He had brought his troubles from London. Living like a parson, he still struggled with his contradictory self, an upright man with a perilous theory. He still dreaded what the world would say if his private thoughts were known.

His pent-up feelings sometimes showed, as on the rare occasions he mooted his evolution heresy to friends. It was criminal, "like confessing a murder," he confided to a colleague, Joseph Hooker. How "absurdly presumptuous" it must seem, he told another; it opens one to "reproach" for being a "complete fool." In 1845, when Sedgwick damned the anonymous evolutionary pot-boiler *Vestiges of the Natural History of Creation* for being subversive and unscientific, Charles read his old professor's review with "fear &

trembling." He had just finished a draft of his own theory and given Emma instructions about publishing it "in case of my sudden death." Maybe he would not survive to see his work in print.[16] In a world full of Sedgwicks maybe this would be just as well.

Events came to a head when Charles had a serious breakdown after his father's death in 1848. Dr. Darwin, an unbeliever, was suffering fiery torments if Emma's favorite scripture were true, but Charles found this incredible. In deepest mourning, he became depressed and severely ill, with violent vomiting, trembling hands, and fainting feelings. For the first time he felt sure that he himself was about to die. Four months at a spa worked wonders, but he returned home only to see his eldest daughter Annie taken sick. As she languished he fortified himself from books by a freethinking theist, Francis Newman. In *The Soul* Newman rejected "the dreadful doctrine of the Eternal Hell," in his spiritual autobiography *Phases of Faith*, Unitarianism. Charles now followed suit. When Annie died tragically in April 1851, aged ten, he found no comfort in Emma's faith.

It was a "bitter & cruel" loss, he told a clerical friend. A week afterwards Charles penned a pathetic vindication of the child, for Emma and himself "in after years, if we live."[17] He remembered Annie as all but perfect, "hardly ever" needing to be "found fault with." "A single glance of my eye, not of displeasure (for I thank God I hardly ever cast one on her) but of want of sympathy would for some minutes alter her whole countenance." Acutely sensitive, she was "never punished in any way whatever," nor did she deserve to be—in this life, let alone the next. Charles, after years of backsliding, had finally broken with Christianity. His father's death had spiked the faith, Annie's clinched the point a fortiori. Eternal punishment was immoral. He would speak out and be damned.

Down House was now his pulpit, evolution the new "gospel."[18] Through sickness and sorrow he pressed on, polishing his theory, extending it, finding illustrations everywhere. He taught himself about species' variability by describing all known barnacles, and in 1853 won the Royal Medal for his efforts, a scientific "knighthood" from the Royal Society of London. He kept fancy pigeons too, developing the analogy between the breeder's selective art and natural selection's far higher "workmanship." Finally in 1856, almost twenty years after conceiving it, he was ready to write up his theory. His confidants—Lyell now, as well as Hooker and Thomas Huxley—egged him on. The time was ripe, his reputation secure.

Huxley, keen to professionalize science and push out the churchmen, baited him with juicy tidbits, like the "indecency" of jellyfish cross-fertilizing through the mouth. Darwin, about to start the *Origin of Species*, shared the lewd jest with Hooker. Nature's depravity cried out against a noble Providence; good grief, Darwin spouted in the next breath, "What a book a Devil's Chaplain might write on the clumsy, wasteful, blundering low & horridly cruel works of nature!"[19]

But he was the apostate now, touting not treachery but a "grander" theology than Anglican creationism. His book would not be a rude parody, mocking God's works, but a paean to the Creator's immutable laws by which the "higher animals" had evolved.

It would have to be. For Darwin had become an establishment figure in his own right, a pillar of the parish. His infants had been christened in Downe church, where the family attended regularly. He himself seldom went, but he gave generously toward church repairs and sent his boys— William, George, Francis, Leonard, and Horace—to be tutored by nearby clergymen. At Downe the priests always had his support; John Brodie Innes, a Tory High Churchman, became a lifelong friend. Together in 1850 they had started a benefit society for the local laborers, with Darwin as guardian. Later Innes made him treasurer of the parish charities, a Coal and Clothing Club and the National School. In 1857, with a testimonial from Innes, Darwin became a county magistrate, swearing on the Bible to keep the Queen's peace, and to "hear and determine divers felonies and also trespasses, and other misdemeanours . . . perpetrated."[20]

Who could despise an evolutionist who pledged himself thus? For all his private fears, Darwin was a public paragon still.

2

A FAMILY DIVIDED

ARWIN'S BOOK, *ON THE ORIGIN OF SPECIES BY MEANS of Natural Selection*, came out in November 1859. Bound in royal green cloth with fine gilt on the spine, it was a smart specimen of Victorian book-making and a superb package for his theory.[1]

The word "evolution" did not appear once in the text but "creation" and its cognate terms were used over one hundred times. At the front, opposite the title, stood a quotation from Lord Bacon on studying God's works as well as his Word, and another by Rev. William Whewell on "general laws" as God's way of working. On the final page, in a mighty flourish, Darwin rhapsodized about the "grandeur" in his view of life. Imagine—all nature's "most beautiful and most wonderful" diversity was the product of the "several powers . . . originally breathed into a few forms or into one"! This was the rhetorical ribbon on the package, but the tone and the terminology—even the pentateuchal "breathed"— were nonetheless sincere. From start to finish the *Origin* was a pious work: "one long argument" against creationist orthodoxy, yes, but equally a reformer's case for creation by natural law.[2]

Of course there was doublethink in it, and a certain subterfuge. The book was the man after all—ambiguous, even contradictory. Darwin dodged human evolution and said nothing about the origin of life or matter. This made the *Origin* safer, less ideological, which was his old strategy. But

he also personified "Nature" as a selector and larded later
editions with quotations from Bishop Butler and "a celebrated author and divine." Here contrivance gave way to
confusion, for these features invited providential readings
even as the rest of the book ruled them out. In the end the
Origin held multiple meanings; it could become all things
to all men.[3]

Radicals loved it, the theology notwithstanding. Darwin's
old tutor Robert Grant, still lecturing at University College,
congratulated him: "With one fell-sweep of the wand of
truth, you have now scattered to the winds the pestilential
vapours accumulated by 'species-mongers.'" Brother Erasmus thought it "the most interesting book" he had ever read,
and relished its Teutonic tendency. "The a priori reasoning
is so entirely satisfactory to me that if the facts wont [sic] fit
in, why so much the worse for the facts is my feeling." Ras's
old dining companion Harriet Martineau, now a notorious
atheist, rejoiced in the *Origin* and dismissed its God-talk as
cheap decoration. How could Darwin possibly have meant
it? His theory, "if true," overthrew "revealed Religion on
the one hand, & Natural (as far as Final Causes & Design
are concerned) on the other."[4]

For all the same reasons Anglican die-hards loathed the
Origin. Darwin's reverend professors were aghast. John
Henslow did credit the book as "a marvellous assemblage
of facts & observations" but slated its author for hubris.
"Darwin attempts more than is granted to Man, just as
people used to account for the origin of Evil—a question
past our finding out." This was mild compared to Adam
Sedgwick, who played the inquisitor to Darwin's infidel in
a long letter thanking him for a copy of the *Origin*. The book
was dangerous, like *Vestiges*; parts "grievously shocked my
moral taste," Sedgwick snarled. If natural selection were
true, "humanity in my mind, would suffer a damage that
might brutalize it—& sink the human race" into a cesspool.
He called himself "a son of a monkey & an old friend of

yours" but then signed off, warning his renegade pupil that "on one condition only . . . we shall meet in heaven": if "you & I" accept God's revelation in nature and the Bible.

This sabre-rattling shocked Emma. She no longer prayed that Charles would escape eternal torments—for her that doctrine had died. What concerned her was his present suffering, the sickness, the anxiety, as the *Origin* went into the world. She still prayed that these pains would make him "look forward . . . to a future state," where their love would go on forever. But Sedgwick's "slashing" letter (as Darwin called it) opened old wounds. She resented it, and refused to show it to the elder daughter Henrietta, let alone her sister Bessy. The Darwin women were of one mind on religion but Henrietta was sixteen and sickly, in no state to suffer from doubting her father's salvation.[5]

Not all Anglicans damned Darwin. The "celebrated author and divine" quoted in later editions of the *Origin* was Rev. Charles Kingsley, novelist, amateur naturalist, and professor of history at Cambridge. His plug for Darwin's theology—it seemed "just as noble" as miraculous creationism—was timely but timid, a mere "yea" to the hearty "amen" from the Oxford geometry professor Rev. Baden Powell. Writing in the Broad Church manifesto *Essays and Reviews*, he declared that the *Origin* "must soon bring about an entire revolution of opinion in favour of the grand principle of the self-evolving powers of nature." For such remarks Powell and his fellow authors were hounded for heresy and two of them eventually prosecuted. In 1861, when a private petition was got up in their defense, Darwin rallied to the cause, adding his signature. He welcomed the efforts of these so-called *septum contra Christum* to "establish religious teaching on a firmer and broader foundation."[6]

Worse heretics embarrassed the Church from without: John Colenso, deposed as a bishop for faulting the Old Testament; Charles Voysey, an unfrocked vicar and founder of the Theistic Church; and Moncure Conway, the maverick

Yankee Methodist who tended London's freethinking South Place Chapel. During the 1860s and 1870s Darwin was asked repeatedly to bankroll them or back their work. But although the *Origin* became all things to all men, he himself found this impossible. Donations, yes; maybe the odd handshake. Otherwise he steered clear of public support for religious heretics—in Great Britain. He was less cautious abroad.

A world away, in the United States, Darwin lent his name to the most extreme religious radicals: a ginger group of lapsed Unitarians and left-wing transcendentalists in the Free Religious Association. In 1871 Francis Abbot, editor of their tabloid weekly *The Index*, sent Darwin sample copies, piquing his interest as well as his sons'. Darwin subscribed immediately and even made generous donations—as much as £25 one year. He read *The Index* avidly, cover-to-cover, and would bait the boys with "the most extraordinary facts" before passing an issue around. But he declined to contribute articles.

Abbot, eager for copy, prodded Darwin with his own pamphlet *Truths for the Times*. Its fifty propositions augured "the extinction of faith in the Christian Confession" and the development of a humanistic "Free Religion" in which "lies the only hope of the spiritual perfection of the individual and the spiritual unity of the race." These were evolutionary "truths" and Darwin responded warmly, "I admire them from my inmost heart & agree to almost every word." Abbot, overjoyed for this one line, obtained Darwin's consent to use it as an advertisement for his tract. For years the blurb appeared in *The Index* alongside rabble-rousing polemics and anti-Christian editorials.[7]

Meanwhile at Downe Darwin's dual life went on. A boorish new vicar named Ffinden took over in 1871 and soon fell out with the family. Charles cut his ties with the village charities; Emma and the daughters left the church for one a couple miles away. The neighbors, fed up with Ffinden too, hardly noticed their absence. The "great folks" in Down House continued to be parish paternalists, keeping up the proprieties. Drunkenness was a problem in the village. Charles had a "horror" of it—two of his relatives had died from alcoholism. With Emma's help he started a temperance reading room in an old school hall, where for a penny a week the local laborers could smoke, play games, and read "respectable" literature, without resorting to the pub.[8] But Ffinden, feeling slighted, interfered constantly and the scheme was never a success.

Nor was such pettiness confined to the parish. The world was full of crotchety curates and bumptious bishops, always meddling with science. Darwin still fretted about offending them unnecessarily. Again he relied on his devout women to help keep the peace.

In 1871 his long-awaited *Descent of Man* came out bearing the imprimatur of daughter Henrietta, an able stylist and fussy moralist. Parts he had feared would read like an infidel sermon—"Who w[oul]d ever have thought I sh[oul]d turn parson"!—and he asked her to tone them down. Emma too had jogged the family censor, reminding her that however "interesting" the book's treatment of morals and religion might be, she would still "dislike it very much as again putting God further off."[9] Henrietta dutifully preened the proofs and the *Descent* caused few commotions. For her good work she was given a fat £30 and a free hand in Charles' biographical sketch of his grandfather Erasmus. These proofs she pruned: *Erasmus Darwin* appeared in 1879 shorn of everything religiously risqué. Even a footnote vanished, the one debunking a story that the old freethinker called for Jesus on his deathbed. Beside her as she snipped was her lawyer husband, an equal moralist, who managed Church property for the Ecclesiastical Commission.[10]

No one curbed Darwin's candor in his own biography. But then it was written for the family, not publication. He had started it in 1876 and now put on the final touches, rounding out his fullest statement ever on "religious belief." At first he had been unwilling to give up Christianity, and had even tried to "invent evidence" to confirm the Gospels, which had prolonged his indecision. But just as his clerical career had died a slow "natural death," so his faith had withered gradually. There had been no turning back once the death-blow fell. His dithering had crystallized into a moral conviction so strict that he could not see how anyone—even Emma—"ought to wish Christianity to be true." If it were, "the plain language" of the New Testament "seems to show that the men who do not believe, and this would include my Father, Brother and almost all my best friends, will be everlastingly punished. And this is a damnable doctrine."

Hard heartfelt words, they recalled the bitter months and years after Dr. Darwin's death. Since then Charles' residual theism had weakened, worn down by controversy. Now as one with "no assured and ever present belief in the existence of a personal God or of a future existence with retribution and reward," he confessed, "I . . . must be content to remain an Agnostic." An unbeliever, yes, but still an upright man, living without the threat of divine wrath. "I feel no remorse from having committed any great sin," he assured Emma and the children. "I believe that I have acted rightly in steadily following and devoting my life to science."[11]

None of this was for circulation—the autobiography would be a posthumous message to the family. Charles entrusted the manuscript to Francis, the son who shared his biological interests. Francis had abandoned a medical career and come to live in the village to work with his father on plants. After his young wife's tragic death in childbirth, he moved into Down House with the baby, Bernard, and sought solace in making a fair copy of the manuscript.[12] Perhaps Francis imagined that one day it would be published.

Charles asked William, the eldest son, to tackle a touchier matter—that blurb in *The Index*. William had married a sister-in-law of one of the Free Religious Association's

founders and, as a banker, had been sending his father's donations to the paper, so he was well placed to intercede. In
June 1880 he asked for the endorsement of *Truths for the
Times* to be scrubbed. He did not explain why, after nine
years, this was necessary, but merely informed Abbot, "My
father . . . had no intention that his words should be used
for this purpose."[13] Abbot complied, though he held a letter proving William wrong. Permission had been granted.

William's intervention, like Henrietta's editing, served to
conceal Charles' identity and restore it to the family. Now,
as his anxious life drew to a close, he was again his own
man, safe at Downe, guarded by loved ones. They knew him
in different ways of course, for he had shown them his separate sides. To the daughters he was the respectable
evolutionist, careful not to offend; to his sons he was the
radical unbeliever whose worst heresies were tucked away
in the autobiography (like they once had been in pocket
notebooks). Emma alone knew him as he knew his own contradictory self, and he was desperate that she should survive
him. With her guidance, the world would know only the
"Darwin" the family chose to reveal.

Why, at this moment, did Darwin retreat? After nine
years, what made him stop his public self-exposure as an
unbeliever, even in the United States? The reason most likely
lay at home. Since the 1850s a militant, working-class movement, Secularism, had been gathering momentum in Britain.
It was full of shameless atheists, eager to poach respectable
support, especially from an eminent scientist. To them Darwin's *Index* blurb would have been fair game.

Charles Bradlaugh, a big boisterous East Ender, was Secularism incarnate. He prowled the country, defying God and
debating churchmen, and edited the movement's "radical
advocate and freethought journal," the *National Reformer*.
The two-penny rag was infamous for preaching "neo-
Malthusianism"—contraception would promote prosper-
ity by reducing the high birth-rate among workers—and in

1877 Bradlaugh and his comrade Annie Besant (an atheist mother-of-two who had left her parson-husband) had actually published do-it-yourself birth control advice, only to be put on trial for the vicious obscenity.[14]

At this point Bradlaugh subpoenaed Darwin, supposing that the author of the *Descent of Man* would back them. Had he not written freely about the reproductive instinct and liberated mankind from superstition? Darwin replied instantly that he was in fact opposed to contraception, not just because it would interfere with natural selection by checking the struggle for existence, but because the practice would "spread to unmarried women." Without the fear of pregnancy, they would become wanton and "destroy chastity on which the family bond depends."[15] Darwin's social sympathies lay, as usual, with Christians, not atheists. He was presumably glad to see the pair found guilty.

That was three years earlier. Now in spring 1880, when William intervened at the *Index*, Bradlaugh had just been returned as a Liberal Member of Parliament. The Christian nation faced the prospect of an avowed atheist and convicted purveyor of "obscenity" swearing on the Bible in order to take his seat in the House of Commons. MPs erupted at the outrage. Atheists were by nature "immoral"; their word meant nothing. Bradlaugh was forbidden to take the oath of allegiance and excluded from the Commons by every trick of parliamentary procedure. Atheism became a burning political issue; the press fanned the flames and soon "Bradlaugh" was a household word. Darwin, mindful of his old subpoena, knew that the MP would want his backing. Removing the *Index* blurb was a wise precaution, to keep it from being appropriated.

Nor was this his only statement that could rebound. Less than two years before he had written to Dr. Edward Aveling, a young anatomy lecturer, thanking him for copies of his articles on evolution and asking to see future installments. Now the series continued in the *National Reformer*

under the title "Darwin and His Works" while Aveling himself stumped the country, stirring up support for Bradlaugh.
In the present political climate what would Aveling make of
his encouraging letter?

In October 1880 Darwin found out when a note from
Aveling came. He was collecting his articles into a book and
asked permission to dedicate it to Darwin. It was to appear
in the "International Library of Science and Freethought"
under the editorship of "my friends Mrs. Annie Besant and
Charles Bradlaugh, M.P."

Darwin replied by return, a four-page letter marked con-
spicuously "Private." No, he would not permit the dedication, "though I thank you for the intended honour." It would
imply "to a certain extent my approval of the general publication," the International Library, "about which I know
nothing," Darwin dissembled, knowing the editors full well.

> Moreover though I am a strong advocate for free thought
> on all subjects, yet it appears to me (whether rightly or
> wrongly) that direct arguments against christianity & the-
> ism produce hardly any effect on the public; & freedom of
> thought is best promoted by the gradual illumination of
> men's minds, which follow[s] from the advance of science.
> It has, therefore, been always my object to avoid writing on
> religion, & I have confined myself to science. I may, how-
> ever, have been unduly biassed by the pain which it would
> give some members of my family, if I aided in any way di-
> rect attacks on religion.

Here spoke one who had been hand-in-glove with Christians all his life, whose entire well-being depended on his
devout wife and daughters. "Gradual illumination" had always been his luxury, religious reticence his practice. He and
Aveling inhabited different worlds.[16]

In August 1881 Bradlaugh hit the headlines again after
winning the by-election called when his seat was declared
vacant. He arrived at the Commons, accompanied by Avel-

ing, only to be barred from entering by the deputy sergeant-at-arms, then dragged down the lobby stairs and flung into Palace Yard by a mob of messengers, policemen, and Tory MPs. In the scuffle Aveling's fountain pen was broken, proving—the hacks cheered—that it was not mightier than the sword. But Bradlaugh's furious vow to "come again with force" set them foaming, and they conjured up scenes of revolution in the evening papers.

Darwin was in town to read them. He was staying a few days with brother Ras, now melancholy and wasted, without the will to live. It was to be their last reunion. Darwin left for Downe knowing that he would "never see such a man again." At home he found Aveling's collected articles, *The Student's Darwin*, minus a dedication, with a note from the author apologizing for his atheistic extrapolations. Darwin replied with a cool thanks, admitting that he could hardly stop writers from taking his views "to a greater length than seems to me safe."[17]

Ras died a fortnight later, an unbeliever, and was buried at Downe on September 1. This "very heavy loss" turned Darwin's thoughts to his own future. All summer he had struggled with despondency, feeling worn out and fearing for his heart (Fig. 1). Having just finished a book on earthworms, he resigned himself to joining them. "I must look forward to Down graveyard as the sweetest place on earth," he sighed to his old colleague Hooker.[18] In this period Darwin thought much on the eternal questions—chance and design, providence and pain—but he now lost no time in putting his earthly affairs in order. There was Ras's estate to administer, a new will to be drawn up—and then on the 27th a telegram came.

It was from Aveling, who was attending the Congress of the International Federation of Freethinkers in London. He wanted to call at Down House the next day with the Congress president, Ludwig Büchner. Darwin could hardly refuse, Aveling or no. Büchner was a renowned physician

whose books sat on Darwin's shelves. He was also a fierce
materialist, like so many German Darwinians, but no worse
than the Jena zoologist Ernst Haeckel, who had visited three
times and upset Emma by ranting. The pair would be welcome for lunch, even though Emma blanched at the thought
of Büchner airing his "very strong religious opinions."[19] To
discourage him she invited the former vicar Brodie Innes.

In the event Büchner was tame and Aveling intense. At
last the thirty-year-old atheist came face-to-face with his
hero. The meal went off without incident but afterwards,
when Darwin adjourned to his old study with Francis and
the two guests, Aveling was primed. Darwin, completely out
of character, pitched in first. "Why do you call yourselves
atheists?" He preferred the word "agnostic," he said. "'Agnostic' was but 'Atheist' writ respectable," Aveling replied,
searching for common ground, "and 'Atheist' was only 'Agnostic' writ aggressive." But, Darwin retorted, "Why should
you be so aggressive?" Is anything to be gained by forcing
new ideas on people? Freethought is "all very well" for the
educated, but are ordinary people "ripe for it"? Here again
spoke the parish naturalist, seeking not to disturb the social
equilibrium.

The atheists realized this, and Aveling rounded on him.
What if the "revolutionary" truth of natural selection had
been addressed only to "the judicious few"? What if he had
delayed publishing the *Origin of Species* until the time was
"ripe"? Had he "kept silence," where would the world be
in 1881? Surely "his own illustrious example" was encouragement to every freethinker to proclaim the truth "abroad
from the house-tops"! Still Aveling missed the real Darwin.
He *had* sat on his theory for twenty years, petrified for his
respectability, upholding the old paternalist order for a generation before publishing the *Origin*.

Only one subject could they all agree on: Christianity.
Darwin admitted that it was not "supported by evidence."
But—he dug at his guests—he had reached this conclusion

only slowly. He did not force new ideas even on himself but waited until the time was ripe. In fact, he told them openly, "I never gave up Christianity until I was forty years of age."[20] It had taken his father's and Annie's deaths to make him shake off the last shreds. And even then he had refused to speak out, or violently to assail people's faith. He never was a comrade-in-arms.

A fortnight later his worm book was published and on April 19, 1882, Darwin succumbed to a heart attack. Emma, Henrietta, and Bessy were present with Francis to hear him whisper, "I am not in the least afraid to die."[21] The other sons, William, George, Leonard, and Horace, rushed home; Brodie Innes offered to perform the burial rites. Everyone at Downe assumed that Charles would be laid to rest, as he had wished, beside Ras in the parish churchyard.

It was not to be. In London Darwin's professional friends began lobbying for a state funeral in Westminster Abbey. A well-connected cousin had the president of the Royal Society, William Spottiswoode, write to ask for the family's permission. A Downe neighbor, the MP Sir John Lubbock, got up a petition in the House of Commons. And Huxley, now Darwin's arch-publicist, put pressure on senior clergymen. Two days after the death was announced he jumped the gun, telling Hooker, "I think the Westminster Abbey business is all settled."

Newspapers latched on to the campaign. Over and over the leader writers insisted that Darwin should not be "laid in a comparatively obscure grave." His "proper place" was among the Abbey's "illustrious dead," whose "reputations are landmarks in the people's history." Was he not the greatest English scientist since Newton? Had he not taught a doctrine quite consistent with "strong religious faith and hope"? True Christians, an Anglican tabloid urged, far from fearing "lest the sacred pavement of the Abbey should cover a secret enemy of the Faith," may rejoice in Darwin's burial

at Westminster as a visible sign of "the reconciliation between Faith and Science."

At Downe the family deliberated. They dreaded "any opposition" to the proposal and scanned the papers with bated
breath. But the pundits spoke as one, the politicians agreed,
and the scientists were adamant: a state funeral it should be.
Emma and William finally consented. It gave them a "pang"
to think that Charles would not be buried where he had lived
and worked for forty years, but on reflection they felt
strongly that he would have "wished to accept" the nation's
"acknowledgement of what he had done."

On April 26, at high noon, the body of Charles Darwin
was borne mightily up the nave of Westminster Abbey by
Huxley, Hooker, and other dignitaries as white-robed choristers sang "I am the resurrection." Behind them in the pro-
cession came the chief mourner, William, and the other children, followed by the elders of science, State, and
Church—"the greatest gathering of intellect . . . ever brought
together in our country," said one. After the service the coffin was carried to the north end of the choir screen, where
the floor was draped with black cloth that dropped into the
dry, sandy grave. Henrietta, Bessy, and the ladies sat down
while the others crowded around (Fig. 2). Anglican priests
rubbed shoulders with agnostic scientists; the Tory leaders
closed ranks with Liberal lords. The coffin was lowered and
the choristers sang "His body is buried in peace, but his
name liveth evermore."[22]

Emma stayed at Downe. She felt closer to Charles there.

3

THE COMPROMISE

"THE CHURCH HAS DARWIN'S CORPSE, BUT THAT IS ALL she can boast. . . . She has not buried Darwin's ideas. They are still at work, sapping and undermining her very foundations." Sentiments like this—the rasp of cloth-cap Secularism—were soon heard following the funeral.

As the body had awaited its place in the Abbey, Charles Bradlaugh was fighting the efforts of Tory Anglicans to bankrupt him, and himself pursuing the deputy sergeant-at-arms for assault. Although duly elected to Parliament a second time, he had still been unable to take his seat, and his case was now a rallying-point for Secularists. Off Fleet Street, the editor of *The Freethinker* was trumpeting Bradlaugh's parliamentary cause. He embellished his paper with a series of blasphemous cartoons that, in July 1882, led to his prosecution and eventual imprisonment as a common criminal.[1] These were the men the Establishment loved to hate; they were pilloried by the very papers that abetted Darwin's burial in the Abbey.

To the Secularists the service smacked of so much hypocrisy and humbug. The "Westminster Abbey business" (as Huxley called it smugly) was pious resurrectionism run amuck. *The Freethinker* retaliated by rumoring that Darwin was a "thorough-going Radical," a "constant and generous supporter of the Bromley Liberal Association" and a public-spirited magistrate who had foiled Lord Stanhope's attempt to close the footpath from Knockholt Beeches across

Chevening Park, a few miles from Downe. So much for the "funny theory . . . that our men of science are nearly all Conservatives." Dr. Edward Aveling, writing in Bradlaugh's *National Reformer*, was bolder: "All Freethinkers hail him as a brother and an ally." While he might not have consciously taken sides, "he was, and will ever be, working with our cause." Aveling chose his words carefully, mindful of his interview at Downe (Fig. 3).[2]

The family members were still in deepest mourning and sensitive to the slightest stain on Darwin's reputation. At first they did not appreciate the threat as the freethinkers staked their claim to the "real" Darwin, the inner man. The Abbey event had been orchestrated so well, the beatification had been so complete—it seemed inconceivable that grubby hands would now attempt a political postmortem. Who would be so callous as to pry into his private life? Darwin had revealed everything that needed to be known about himself. The rest concerned only his loved ones. Downe cast a protective cloak around his intimate life and views. Darwin had planned it like that, secure in the knowledge that he was unreachable except on his own terms.

The family assumed that it would continue that way. They imagined that his public image—as the respectable parish naturalist—would be theirs to project. His identity was to be as closely guarded as his daily existence had been the forty years since he fled London, a nervous young husband with his heretical evolutionary thoughts tucked away in pocket notebooks.

In this belief, the Darwins began to collect and recollect—letters, sayings, memorabilia. The process went on for months, accompanied by many a pang. They had barely begun when more tragedy struck. Within days of her master's death, Polly, the family's fox terrier, became ill. Her throat swelled and, heartbroken, she crept away several times as if to die. At Emma's request, Francis silenced her mournful bark with prussic acid, the humane method his father had devised to sacrifice pigeons. They buried her in a hillock beneath an apple tree out in the orchard. She was one part of the past that would not return to haunt them.

For Henrietta, who had left Polly at Downe on getting married, the loss could not have come at a worse time. In grief, she now poured herself into a chronicle of her father's final illness, ending with a minute account of his last hour.[3] Her sister Bessy made no record of her emotions, which must have been intense, but the sons, with an eye on posterity, produced hefty reminiscences. They were the keepers of Darwin's scientific persona, and Francis—who had worked closely with his father on plants—now took on the job of preparing a *Life and Letters*. This literary headstone, the expected tribute to all men great and good, had to be erected without delay. He threw himself into the task, working from his father's study at Downe, where he and his little son Bernard remained with Emma.

The house felt empty now, despite the boisterous five-year-old. A glorious spring and summer passed, but the gardens looked run down. Life had lost its radiant center. Emma was bereft (Fig. 4). "Oh, how I miss my daily fixed occupation," she sighed to Leonard. And to Henrietta, "It often comes over me with a wave of desolate feeling that there is nothing I need do." Each familiar experience—the early breakfast, the visit to the garden, the train to London—became freshly poignant, undertaken alone.

Emma soothed herself by jotting down fond memories and re-reading Charles' letters. "I have not found many," she told William, "we were so seldom apart, and never I think for the last 15 or 20 years." All that she had dated from the 1850s and earlier. Illness was their central theme, but this was swathed in tender feelings and brought back memories of the children. As she read, she found the note written one stormy afternoon shortly after her mother died. "I have been sitting in [the] summer-house, whilst watching the thunder-storms," Charles consoled her, "& thinking

what a fortunate man I am, so well off in worldly circumstances, with such dear little children . . . & far more than
all with such a wife." He had "never heard a word" pass
her lips that was better left unsaid, and felt sure that he
would still "say so on my death-bed,—bless you my dear
wife." Emma remembered his "special words" to her just
before the end: his prophecy had come true.[4]

The letters were a comfort in her loneliness. She kept them
in a "precious packet" that stayed with her wherever she
went. They helped her feel close to him again, just as she
had when everyone else was at the funeral. He belonged to
the parish, to Downe, to her—not to the world outside. She
had protected him all those years. She had been so much
more than the bearer of his children and a nurse to his physical suffering. When at last he relinquished the comforts and
terrors of Christianity, she became his means of grace. Like
a saintly mother, she felt for him, prayed for him. Insensi-
bly, he grew to depend on her faith and intuitions; they made
up for that part of his religious sentiment eroded by reason
and bitter grief. Now he was with her still, and would always be. Of this she felt sure.

> Yet less of sorrow lives in me
> For days of happy commune dead,
> Less yearning for the friendship fled
> Than some strong bond which still shall be.

Her favorite lines from Tennyson's *In Memoriam* said it all.[5]

But when autumn came, Emma's sad reverie was rudely
broken. So was everyone else's. The scientific world knew
that Francis had been amassing materials for the *Life and
Letters*, so no one imagined that a trusted colleague would
rush ahead and publish private correspondence without the
family's permission[6]—much less publish a letter of such exquisite sensitivity as appeared on the afternoon of September 23 in the *Pall Mall Gazette*.

It was Darwin's reply to a religious query from a young German count, a student of Ernst Haeckel's at Jena. Haeckel, the crusading zoologist who descended three times on Down House as Darwin's guest, had acquired the letter. On the 18th, in an address to a German scientific congress, he read a translation from the platform. The next morning it was splashed all over the German papers. British freethinkers gleefully fell on this evidence and retranslated the text into English. The back-to-back translations meant that a dubious version of Darwin's private views was paraded before the very London intelligentsia who had given him a Christian burial in the Abbey. And it revealed Darwin as a complete unbeliever.[7] No, he did not believe "that any Revelation has ever been made." "With regard to a future life," he added, "every one must draw his conclusions from vague and conflicting probabilities."

Actually, the translations did not misrepresent the original, as subsequent inquiries showed.[8] Haeckel had exposed not only Darwin; he had lifted the veil surrounding his oldest and deepest conflict with Emma, over their eternal destiny together.

But the real problem was the use made of the letter in England. The *National Reformer* reprinted the translation on October 1. Later that month Bradlaugh twisted the knife with a front-page correspondence between Haeckel and Aveling. This pointed up the hypocrisy of England's leading scientific journal, *Nature*, which had translated Haeckel's address verbatim, but replaced the letter with an ellipsis. The feelings of "friends and relatives," growled Aveling, had become a pretext for avoiding these "unpleasant facts." In the same issue, and the next, he capitalized on Haeckel's revelation by publishing a full-blown account of his own visit to Down House the previous autumn with that other Teutonic freethinker, Ludwig Büchner. This, too, was front-page fare, battering down the door of Darwin's domestic life, regardless of personal cost to the family.

Aveling described the scene that had greeted him: Mr. and Mrs. Darwin, Francis, and some small children were present for lunch, as was "a clergyman of the English Church," who sat beside Mrs. Darwin. Tackled on religion afterwards, their host said that he preferred to be called an agnostic, rather than atheist. And he admitted that he had given up Christianity at the age of forty. Aveling was ecstatic. "I, like the rest of the outside world, was not sure as to his position in regard to religion. Now, from his own lips, I knew that . . . the step taken by so many of us had been taken by him long ago. What a strength and hope are in the thought that the first thinker of our age had abandoned Christianity."[9]

Emma dreaded publicity. She had feared it all summer, ever since Francis began sifting correspondence for the *Life and Letters*. Now the worst had happened. This exposure by rank infidels really was beyond the pale. How many more letters would return to haunt them? How could the family protect itself and safeguard Father's memory?[10] If only she could bury the religious parts of the past, like little Polly; or at least bury them deep in her own heart.

The *Life and Letters* was to be based on Darwin's autobiography, the private narrative begun in 1876 and written for the family. Francis, who was entrusted with the manuscript, had copied it out laboriously in his rounded, legible hand in the aftermath of his wife's death. Emma now toothcombed Francis's copy. In October 1882 she set down an interdict next to the most sensitive passage, in the section on "religious belief." Here Darwin had declared his innermost thoughts. He failed to see how anyone "ought to wish Christianity to be true," given its "damnable doctrine" that unbelievers such as his father, his brother, and "almost all" his best friends stood to be "everlastingly punished." Emma, for her part, could not see why anything so emotive and ill-expressed should appear in print. "It seems to me raw," she wrote. "Nothing can be said too severe upon the doctrine of everlasting punishment for disbelief—but very few w[oul]d call that 'Christianity,' (tho' the words are there)."

Emma was arguing with herself as well as Francis. The words *were* there, the words in the Gospel of John that she had commended to Charles when they were about to be married. It was she who had written in a letter to him shortly afterwards—a "beautiful letter," he called it in the autobiography—"I should be most unhappy if I thought we did not belong to each other forever." And now, she knew, he had often "kissed & cryed over this," especially when he thought of Annie. He said so in a note on her letter, which he had treasured and preserved all those years.[11] But believe in a religion of eternal punishment he could never do— not since the loss of Annie and the death of Dr. Darwin. It was Emma's notion of Christianity that had changed, not his.

The next autumn Francis remarried and went to live near his brothers George and Horace in Cambridge. Emma too had bought a house there, to be near the children during the winter months. Left to his own devices for most of the year in this growing Darwin enclave—five more grandchildren were born in Cambridge by the time the *Life and Letters* appeared —Francis decided to publish the autobiography more or less complete, including the section on religious belief. But when the first proofs arrived in 1885 bitter feelings erupted. The "damnable" passage that had upset Emma was evidently only one of many to cause offense. Others in the section on religious belief were almost as bad, and the attempts to censor them now caused a sharp rift in the family.

Henrietta and her lawyer husband on the Ecclesiastical Commission would not countenance publication. Even litigation could not be ruled out if Francis and his brothers went ahead with the religious section intact. It was political dynamite. It assailed "the faith of England," Henrietta snapped, and would undermine people's beliefs. Parents would have to keep it from their children. Its rash statements would incite public discussions and dissensions. It would

grieve Emma, something that Father himself had been careful to avoid during his lifetime. Leonard chimed in that Father would as soon have "burnt his hand off" as write anything to cause Mother pain. Lenny was of a mind to
compromise. The autobiography was a "private document,"
but let parts of it be released. Then the public would have
"absolutely no right to enquire further."[12]

Francis was nettled and nonplussed. Charles had seldom
spoken on religious subjects. He gave his sons to believe that
this was because he and their mother did not see eye to eye.
"These are very difficult matters. You must settle them for
yourselves," he was remembered saying. Religion was
woman's realm in the Darwin household, and the daughters
and sons had long suppressed their differences. Henrietta's
"considerable boiling overy state of mind," as Francis called
it with a sexist twist, was as startling as it was predictable.
Her red-lining of the Erasmus Darwin biography in 1879
was evidently motivated by the same deep-seated scruples
that now convulsed the family. And these "conservato-grundiform feelings" were apparently shared by her husband,
"bless his heart," Francis sneered to William.[13] Only by appealing indirectly through Emma, the one who was in touch
with both sides, Henrietta's and the boys', could the *Life
and Letters* now be spared.

"If the Religious part is not published," Francis told his
mother, "I shall be absolutely bound to say that it has been
omitted . . . and I do not believe that Father would like it."
It seemed shabby and would reflect badly on Father's open,
honest image. Anyway, Francis reminded her, the worst had
already come out: "It does not seem worthy of him that his
views (on what he certainly thought strongly ab[ou]t) should
only be made known through men such as Aveling, and
through Haeckel who published the letter illegally and
against our wishes." Publishing the religious section sub-
stantially intact would reinstate their father's integrity. The
subject had to be freed from the clutches of the freethinkers

and brought back under family control. Moreover, by allowing Father to speak for himself, "many who cannot believe in the old faith and yet feel it wicked to doubt" may be comforted. "If they are to be led by anybody, they may do worse than be led by a great man" whose life was "absolutely pure and honourable," who wrote about his religious views "with simple truthfulness" and, in the end, was—as he said—"content to remain an Agnostic."[14]

Emma's response was conciliatory, though she felt that the "whole" religious section was "not what the world will think worthy of the highest powers of his mind." She cringed at the "dogmatic" passages with their "tone of contempt" for Christian beliefs. How would "your father's religious friends" react, to say nothing of the devout "old servants"? Eventually, by mid-1885, the compromise was struck. And not a moment too soon for family members—minus Emma—to attend the unveiling of the Darwin statue in the Natural History Museum at South Kensington. The autobiography was dismembered, the section on religious belief was removed to a separate chapter in the *Life and Letters*, and only "extracts, somewhat abbreviated," were printed. All reference in the autobiography to internal family relations—to the marriage, to Annie's death, to domestic life at Downe—was expunged.[15]

In 1886 the *Life and Letters* went to press as Bradlaugh sat in the Commons for the first time, triumphant over "conservato-grundiform feelings" of a similar sort. Atheism was at last grudgingly recognized in public life, even if it was a long way from respectable. The next October, as the first self-confessed atheist at Westminster pushed through his bill permitting members to "affirm" rather than swear the parliamentary oath, Francis's three-volume monument went on sale for almost two pounds—a week's wages for a well-paid worker. Four thousand copies sold in a month, making it a best-seller.[16]

The family's "Darwin" appears as a modest, hesitant agnostic who reluctantly gave up Christianity for lack of historical evidence. No inkling is given of his guilty pleasures in materialist *bon mots* in the early notebooks, his fears of persecution, or his veiled self-reference as a "Devil's Chaplain." The "damnable" passage has vanished. Haeckel's letter is included, transcribed properly, but so too is every scrap of countervailing testimony Francis could muster—anything that would point to the tempered respectability of his father's religious views.

Aveling, Darwin's would-be alter-ego, the thirty-year-old infidel who had sought to extract an atheistic confession, is dealt with summarily in a footnote. He "gives quite fairly his impression of my father's views," Francis conceded, having been present at their meeting. But he seems "to regard the absence of aggressiveness in my father's views as distinguishing them in an unessential manner from his own." Here Francis, no less than Emma and Henrietta, drew the line— the line separating respectability from ill-breeding. "In my judgment, it is precisely differences of this kind which distinguish him so completely from the class of thinkers to which Dr. Aveling belongs."[17]

It was Darwin's "class of thinkers"—the professional gentlemen—who buried him in the Abbey. They were the ones who could boast, as Darwin did in the autobiography, of feeling "no remorse from having committed any great sin." Francis printed this self-exculpation on the last page of the *Life and Letters*, though Henrietta objected "insanely."[18] To him the remark seemed modest and fair, an epitaph for the "great man" whose life had been "absolutely pure and honourable."

When Secularists had finished the book, they disagreed categorically. They, like Aveling, had thought Darwin a "brother" and an "ally"; now he suddenly appeared a reprobate.

In 1888 the Freethought Publishing Company began circulating a savage, four-penny *Indictment of Darwin*. This was Bradlaugh's company, and it looked like revenge for Darwin's refusal to support him in the 1877 obscenity trial.

The pamphlet was essentially a review of the *Life and Letters*. Charging Darwin with pusillanimity and prevarication, it concluded that he had lapsed from unbelief. The priests and their pyre had scared him off:

> Mr. Darwin was not purely and simply in religious matters a simpleton. He was a hypocrite and he knew it; he tried to smother his qualms. . . . For he saw that the black beasts [i.e., priests] and their wood were no mere relics of the past. He feared, he propitiated, he won. And his body was placed within the four walls of Westminster Abbey in London—not scattered to the four winds of the Campo di Fiori in Rome. And the black beasts sang his praise.[19]

Harsh, perhaps, but it was more accurate as an assessment of Darwin's identity than anything Secularists had written before. He had indeed "feared" exposure, but he had made his peace with the Establishment and "won" his place in the Abbey. This was not the strategy of a "hypocrite," much less a "simpleton." It was not really a strategy at all. To an English gentleman, discretion came automatically. There was no public show; he had simply moved with the times to a polite agnosticism.

Only Emma knew what a terrible, tortuous journey it had been.

1 *Darwin—the last photograph*

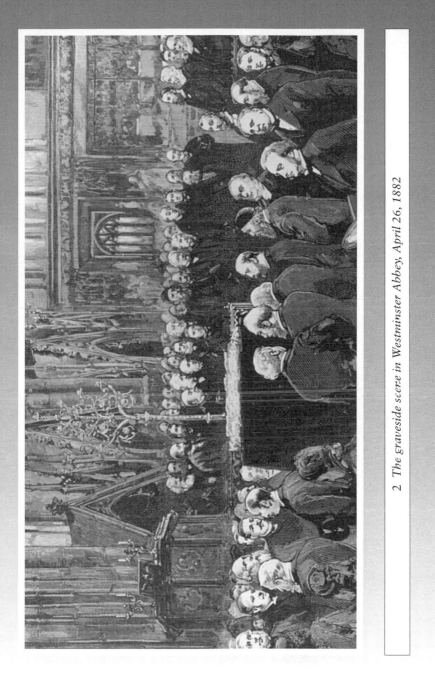

2 *The graveside scene in Westminster Abbey, April 26, 1882*

3 *The secular sun of the nineteenth century:*
Darwin banishing bishops, Bibles, and priestly hobgoblins

4 *Emma Darwin at the time of Charles' death*

5 *Rev. John Mutch*
   (1852–97)

6 *Lady Hope*
   in her prime

7 Mr. Fegan goes camping: seaside bivouacs prepared his boys for "hiving off" to Canada

8 Lady Hope's coffee tent for hop pickers

9 *A. T. Robertson at Northfield in 1915*

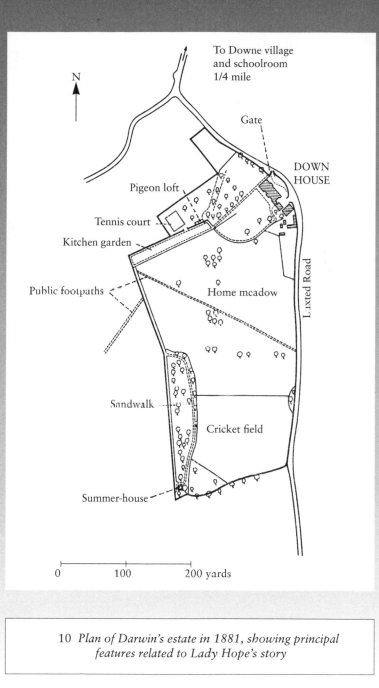

N

To Downe village
and schoolroom
1/4 mile

Gate

DOWN
HOUSE

Pigeon loft

Tennis court

Kitchen garden

Public footpaths

Home meadow

Lixted Road

Sandwalk

Cricket field

Summer-house

0   100   200 yards

10 *Plan of Darwin's estate in 1881, showing principal
features related to Lady Hope's story*

11 *Down House from the garden at the time of Darwin's death: Lady Hope described the view out the second-floor bay window*

12 *Darwin's summer-house at the south end of the Sandwalk*

13 *Monument to an indomitable matron: Lady Hope's headstone towers over the surrounding graves in the Anglican cemetery at Rookwood in suburban Sydney*

DARWIN'S LAST HOURS

DARWIN

"*The Believer*"

By Oswald J. Smith

DARWIN'S BURIAL PLACE

Charles Darwin's Deathbed.

IN 1871 was published Charles Darwin's famous book, *The Descent of Man*, which created a furore in the religious world.

It presented his speculations on the probable ancestry of man. He traced the descent of the human race back to an ape-like creature, and still further back until he reached the speck of protoplasm containing in itself, as he supposed, all those evolutionary potentialities, which after centuries of slow advancement resulted in man. However,

15 *Leonard, aged 80,*
the last of the Darwin children

16 *Sir Arthur Keith (standing on verandah) and Dr. George Buckston Browne (seated with moustache) at the Down House opening ceremony, June 7, 1929*

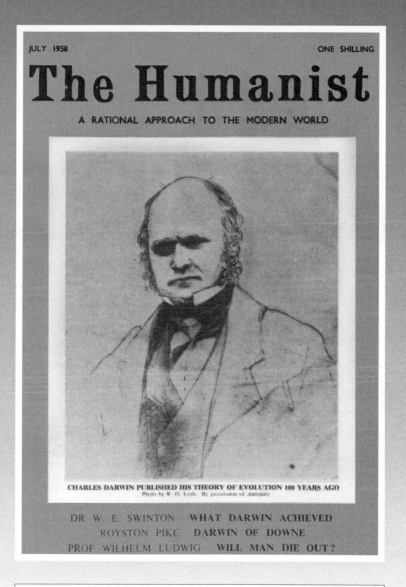

JULY 1958   ONE SHILLING

The Humanist

A RATIONAL APPROACH TO THE MODERN WORLD

CHARLES DARWIN PUBLISHED HIS THEORY OF EVOLUTION 100 YEARS AGO
Photo by R. G. Leah. By permission of *Antiquity*

DR W. E. SWINTON   WHAT DARWIN ACHIEVED
ROYSTON PIKE   DARWIN OF DOWNE
PROF WILHELM LUDWIG   WILL MAN DIE OUT?

17   *The commemorative issue where latter-day secularists tackled the "myth" of Darwin's "deathbed conversion"*

4

EVANGELICAL
INNUENDOES

D ARWIN WAS A COVETED ALLY. SECLUDED AT DOWNE,
religiously elusive and scientifically eminent, he cut
the figure of a detached, objective researcher. Ac-
cordingly, he was appealed to, deferred to, and co-opted by
all manner of groups seeking validation for their views. He
was tugged this way and that, by fellow scientists, the London intelligentsia, the militant atheists. Then the *Life and
Letters* bolstered his respectability by concealing the depth
of his unbelief. And the result was a minor Darwin legend,
created by the family itself. The world was denied knowledge of his real religious views for seventy years, until an
unexpurgated version of the autobiography came out.[1]

Yet the family was not omnipotent. They could not prevent others with inside knowledge from embroidering it for
their own ends. Aveling's opportunism had been thwarted.
But rumors about Darwin were now to spread from the opposite, religious, quarter, enough to unsettle the family
again, although not, mercifully, until after Emma's own
death in 1896.

The autobiography was unequivocal: Darwin no longer
regarded himself as a Christian. The offending 1879 letter
confirmed as much. But it could always be claimed that he
had recanted at the last moment, as he faced death. Such
deathbed conversion stories were the stock-in-trade of evangelical propaganda. From Spinoza, Voltaire, and Tom Paine
right up to Bradlaugh himself, great unbelievers had been

routinely traduced by sanctimonious busybodies, who imagined that fear of dying would turn even the most obdurate sinners toward salvation. This was no doubt one reason why Henrietta took pains to detail her father's final hour and why Francis published as one of Darwin's last utterances: "I am not the least afraid to die."[2] It was part of the family's overall strategy—to ward off the religious vultures.

But to no avail. Neither the *Life and Letters* nor anything else the family published sufficed to stop the sneaking suspicion that Darwin underwent a deathbed conversion. For over a century it has remained a persistent rumor within evangelical circles on both sides of the Atlantic. Not infrequently an obscure tract or an odd page in a devotional book is the only evidence offered. All these sources manifestly depend on each other, so often has the story been recycled. And most of them credit a woman who claimed to have visited and spoken with Darwin before he died, Lady Hope.

Of course tales about Darwin on his deathbed began to circulate long before Lady Hope spoke out. They were apparently as baseless as they were harmless. The earliest reference to a "last confession of faith," in a sermon preached by a "Mr Huntingdon" in Tenby parish church, south Wales, a few days after the Abbey funeral, passed largely unnoticed.[3] Equally inane was the report a few months later from a Yorkshire vicar who claimed to have seen a letter addressed to his uncle, the Glasgow divinity professor John Eadie, in which Darwin said that "he can with confidence look to Calvary."[4]

In January 1887, however, a strange query from a journalist on the Toronto *Mail* reached Francis Darwin via Huxley. Was it true, as a local parson had preached, that "Mr Darwin, when on his death-bed, abjectly whined for a minister and renouncing Evolution, sought safety in the blood of the Saviour"? The parson was Rev. John Mutch of Chalmers Presbyterian Church, a large and flourishing Toronto congregation (Fig. 5). On what authority he made his astonishing remark—if, indeed, the *Mail*'s report was true—is uncertain. A graduate of the University of Toronto, Mutch was an earnest, some thought feisty, evangelical. He was thirty-five years old, in his first charge, and specially concerned with young people. Since Darwin's colleague Alfred Russel Wallace was due in town in early February, to address university students on "the Darwinian theory," Mutch possibly felt called upon to strike preemptively with a bit of holy fabrication. This was Francis's view, although he knew nothing of Mutch; and he authorized Huxley to state that the report was "false and without any kind of foundation."[5] The matter ended there.

Or so it would seem. For despite the fantastic implausibility of the Toronto story, one wonders how it could have arisen—almost five years after Darwin's death and so far from Downe. Suppose that Mutch was not fabricating: instead, he was adding a grotesque twist to tales of Darwin's spiritual state filtering over from England. Could such transatlantic tittle-tattle have reached him? Where would it have originated? Can the story of Darwin on his deathbed be traced back to a particular person? The Darwin family never took such questions seriously. If they had, they might not have been caught out in later years. The same goes for all the establishment figures since Darwin's day who have pooh-poohed the power of evangelicalism.

In fact, the origins of the story lie deep in the maelstrom of metropolitan revivals that swept Britain and America in the late nineteenth century. The key evangelists of the era were Americans, D. L. Moody and Ira Sankey, a gifted duo, like their English contemporaries Gilbert and Sullivan: Moody adept with words, Sankey on the harmonium. They attracted massive crowds on both sides of the Atlantic. In April 1875, while Darwin visited his brother Erasmus in London's West End, Moody and Sankey were packing the Agricultural Hall in Islington every night with audiences of 15,000 or more. Six years later, as Darwin bid farewell to

Aveling and Büchner and published his book on worms, the Americans were repeating their performance in the cities of Scotland. The second mission ended in London with eight months of meetings in 1883–84.

Everywhere they went, Moody and Sankey were courted by the well-to-do, once it was seen how effectively they pacified unbelief, reformed manners, and invigorated the churches. Generous support for both missions came from T. Anthony Denny, an Irish-born Presbyterian philanthropist. Having made his fortune in pork, he larded the coffers of many evangelical enterprises, especially the Salvation Army.[6] In the Moody circle was another distinguished Irishman, Robert Anderson, a member of the ultra-low church Plymouth Brethren and a polished barrister. He was running Home Office undercover operations against Fenian "dynamiters" and would soon take over the Criminal Investigation Department at Scotland Yard during the "Jack the Ripper" murders.[7] Military men were part of the circle. One was General Sir Arthur Cotton of the Royal Engineers, whose life-work was the irrigation of southern India; he introduced his daughter Elizabeth, whose life-work was the iniquities of drink.[8]

Elizabeth is the key to the story. An eldest child, she grew up in the far corners of the Empire and learned the art of leadership at home from the man who wrung more revenue out of the Madras plantations than any previous administrator. The general's health began to fail in the mid-1850s and the family returned to England. They settled for a time near Beckenham in Kent, a few miles from Downe, then moved from place to place in search of a salubrious home. When Elizabeth turned eighteen, in 1860, and the general retired, she served faithfully as his aide-de-camp in all evangelical activities. About 1870 the family settled permanently in Dorking, not far from the Darwins' Wedgwood relatives.[9]

Immediately Elizabeth and the general set out to evangelize the district. Being Anglicans, they targeted working-class families who would not attend the parish church. Sunday school sessions led to weekday meetings for children in rented rooms, which led in turn to home visits with mothers for Bible-reading and prayer. The fathers were usually in the pubs. These "dens of iniquity" with their "poisonous miasma" were attacked in 1873 by Elizabeth and the general. They offered a wholesome alternative: a "coffee-room," where the men would renounce smoking, card-playing, billiards, and bad language in exchange for simple nourishment, spiritual and physical. The coffee-room was a success and, as the ministry grew, the idea caught on.[10] Soon Elizabeth was spreading the good news around the country under Moody and Sankey's banner.

The result was fame, influence, and marriage. By July 1875, when the Americans' first mission ended, Elizabeth had become an accredited evangelical activist. She was close to Moody and his family; she certainly knew Denny and Anderson. Another of her new friends connected with the Moody circle was Admiral Sir James Hope, a sixty-nine-year-old widower, who shared her concern for drunkenness. At thirty-five Elizabeth was rather eligible (or rather vain); she married him in December 1877 and moved to his estate in Scotland.

Now known as Lady Hope of Carriden, Elizabeth continued her ministry with a noble sense of duty (Fig. 6). In pubs and schoolrooms, cottages and castles, she preached and prayed and read the Bible, with drunkards, the destitute, and the dying. Month by month she sent back anecdotes of the work to her little flock in Dorking, and sometimes she came down to visit them. From Dorking she would go farther afield. Kentish villages held a special attraction for her, those in the hop-growing district around Westerham, Sevenoaks, and Sundridge, where she once visited Darwin's colleague William Spottiswoode, president of the Royal Society. Back in Beckenham, in February 1881, she opened a new coffee-house and mission room.[11]

All these village haunts lay within a few miles of Downe. Dorking itself was only fifteen miles away and visited by Darwin yearly from 1873 to 1880. But if Lady Hope ever met Darwin, as she later claimed, it was on his home ground. And she did not barge into Downe on a day's notice, like Aveling and Büchner; she insinuated herself, or perhaps was introduced.

Her entrée was a young friend of Denny's and Anderson's, a member of the Irish Plymouth Brotherhood named James Fegan. They got acquainted before her marriage, probably during the latter phase of Moody's first mission. Fegan had been with a London brokerage firm until he came of age, in 1873, when he went into tent preaching and rescuing street urchins. He founded a string of city homes for boys and, to brighten their lives, he invented—or so he claimed—"camping out"(Fig. 7).[12] Tents had several uses. Each summer the boys would accompany Fegan to the Kentish countryside where they would pitch tents and enjoy a holiday. Fegan would pitch his own tent and preach to the locals. Kent was then the hop-growing heartland of England. In August and September every year, tens of thousands of working people came down from the poorer quarters of London to pick hops for a pittance. Drunkenness was a problem, and all that went with it.[13] In the rich harvest years of the early 1880s Fegan did his bit to keep the peace.

The camping program started after Fegan's parents moved out of London in 1879. They took a house called "Laurel Grove" in Downe. But early in 1880 Fegan's father died and was buried in the parish churchyard. Despite responsibility for the orphanages, Fegan went to live with his stricken mother. He conceived the idea of bringing his boys out for a visit. They arrived in Downe that summer, sixty-seven lads from darkest Deptford, and they stayed in tents until the end of August. Just before they left, Fegan led them along Luxted Road, a quarter-mile south of the village, where Down House stood. He had a word at the door, and when

Darwin and the household emerged, the boys assembled on the front lawn and sang a few hymns. Their reward was sixpence each—in all, nearly two pounds—which they acknowledged with ringing cheers before trooping back to the village.

Darwin, it happened, had been in the middle of a letter to his friend Brodie Innes, the former vicar. He sat back down to report uneasily on the "curious scene." Imagine a bunch of "half-reformed criminals & vagabond boys" invading the village for a "holiday." There were some "very good faces" but others were "atrociously bad." And, talking of such, "did you see in the papers an account of a burglary at High-Elms," Sir John Lubbock's mansion on the other side of the village? It was a "bad one." The thieves tried to break into the butler's pantry; the butler was inside "unarmed." "I wish I had got your rockets for this house," Darwin ended, to which Innes replied with the name of a gunmaker in Pall Mall.[14]

But there was nothing for the local gentry to fear—the lads were held in leash. Fegan resumed tent-preaching after they left. Week by week, at Bromley, Orpington, and nearerby, hundreds turned out to hear him. In Downe he distributed "scarlet play bills . . . announcing his performances in the 'big tent' in Osborne's field—twice on Sunday and once *every* ev[enin]g"—and many were converted.[15] When autumn came, and the days grew shorter, Fegan sought a permanent base of operations. He asked for the old schoolroom at Downe, where the Darwin family had set up a temperance reading room for the village laborers after falling out with Ffinden. Darwin, who rented the room from Lubbock, replied warmly to Fegan's request:

> You have more right to it than we have, for your services have done more for the village in a few months than all our efforts for many years. We have never been able to reclaim a drunkard, but through your services I do not know that there is one drunkard left in the village.[16]

The services continued in the schoolroom. Fegan lived and worked in Downe throughout the winter and, indeed, for two more years before moving away. The Darwins remained impressed. "Hurrah for Mr. Fegan!" Emma exclaimed to Henrietta in February 1881 on hearing that a notorious local drunk had been converted. Parslow, the family's old butler, was also "brought into church membership," as was Mrs. Sales, their housekeeper. In later years, when Fegan returned to Downe for a mission, the Darwins altered their dinner hour so that the servants could attend.[17]

In early July 1881 Fegan collapsed from heatstroke and went away to convalesce. During his three-month absence— by October he was again preaching to "crowded congregations" at Downe—someone was needed to carry on his village mission, particularly as 2,500 laborers were about to descend on the surrounding parishes for hop picking.[18] Fegan's stand-in would need to be firm and disciplined, used to pitching tents in the face of adversity. A military background would help. It is likely that Lady Hope was his fill-in. Her husband had died in Scotland early the previous month; she now made Dorking her home again, with the general and her mother. And there is evidence of her connection with Fegan's ministry in the area about this time. She left a detailed, anecdotal account of tent evangelism among the Kent hop-pickers and the setting up of a "coffee tent" for these migrants in the region where "our friend" Fegan worked (Fig. 8).[19]

She also reported meeting Darwin in the autumn of 1881. This story did not appear in print for thirty-four years, but it was possibly the origin of all the post-1882 deathbed stories. If it spread, it was by word of mouth among English evangelicals and their American friends. From these circles the gossip could easily have spun out to reach Rev. John Mutch in Toronto by 1887. Maybe Fegan repeated it when in 1884 he first took some of his boys to a settlement home in Toronto. Maybe Moody himself repeated it in 1886 at

his college summer school in East Northfield, Massachusetts, where students from the University of Toronto were
present. Maybe the Scottish evangelist James Scroggie heard
about Darwin from Lady Hope when they worked together
in Moody's second London mission, and then embellished
her account for the sake of his relative, Rev. Mutch.[20] None
of these transatlantic pathways can be discounted.

Whatever the case, there is no doubt that Lady Hope was
making discreet comments about Darwin to her religious
friends long before the story was published. After her husband's death, she kept up a whirlwind of temperance work,
retailing her experiences in the guise of tracts and edifying
novels. This was religious entrepreneurship on a scale
appropriate to an admiral's legacy and a general's pension.
But in 1893 she became the third wife of the pork philanthropist T. A. Denny, who was only twenty-four years her
elder. She acquired £75,000 capital as a marriage settlement
and a London address to match. The drawing rooms of the
evangelical elite now became her haunts, and it was there
that she became the confidante of the capital's top detective,
Robert Anderson, head of Scotland Yard.

The Andersons in Notting Hill and the Dennys in Mar-
ble Arch were almost neighbors. Dinner parties, with Bible-
readings afterwards, brought them together in each other's
homes. It was on some such occasion that Lady Hope spoke
to Anderson about visiting Darwin. In 1907 he vouched for
her story, touching on it in a tantalizing footnote to one of
his religious books: "a friend of mine who was much with
Darwin during his last illness assures me that he expressed
the greatest reverence for the Scriptures and bore testimony
to their value."[21]

But Lady Hope's credibility was running out—it was going
every bit as fast as the new motor car she bought in 1906.
Deception was not her downfall, but rather the capacity of
being deceived. She lacked the talent for religious big business. "Remember," the admiral had warned her in a codicil

to his will, "that no income will prove sufficient to keep you out of debt unless you learn to keep some kind of account and exercise a proper control over your Expenditure."

Her second husband, now elderly and frail, was increasingly unable to manage his fortune. Fearful of his eternal destiny, he gave money away left and right, a "colossal fire insurance," according to his sons, who saw their inheritance being frittered away. Lady Hope, whom they already resented for not calling herself by their family name, seems to have been the main beneficiary. She got another £75,000 to open a huge hostel for servants in the Edgware Road, but it flopped. She secretly started a "river club" to cater for down-and-outs along the Thames, which shocked her husband when he found out. After he died in 1909, she lost the hostel's lease to her stepsons and fell on hard times. She exchanged a patent on a hat pin for shares that never had any value. She entrusted her affairs to a gentleman who, she claimed in court, defrauded her. *The Times* carried the humiliating story of her bankruptcy proceedings in 1911. Having forfeited all the income from both her husbands' wills, she was living on £10 per week with £14,000 in liabilities. The Denny sons came forward with £4,000 "for the benefit of the creditors" and in May 1912 their stepmother was discharged.[22]

Scandal dogs those who preach moral rectitude, and Lady Hope was no exception. Now seventy, with little but a secondhand title to her name, she retreated to New York City in the summer of 1913 and began preaching in the missions of the Bowery and Chinatown. She wanted to set up a "club for inebriates" like the ones she had established in England. From New York she sashayed up and down the Atlantic seaboard, putting in an appearance the next autumn at Newport, Rhode Island, where she was feted by local socialites. Then in 1915, three years after her fall from grace in England, she steeled herself to visit the Moody family in Massachusetts. Moody had died, and she knew her own days were numbered. Breast cancer had just been diagnosed.[23]

5

LADY HOPE'S STORY

ADY HOPE ARRIVED IN EAST NORTHFIELD, MASSACHU-setts, at the beginning of August 1915 for the largest of the summer conferences held annually at North-field Seminary, the girls' preparatory school founded by D. L. Moody. It was a miserable, rainy week. None of the English guest speakers had shown up; they were detained by illness or the War.[1] Professor A. T. Robertson of Southern Baptist Theological Seminary in Louisville, Kentucky, helped make up for the loss in his morning Bible classes (Fig. 9). There he expounded the Epistle to the Hebrews from the original Greek, applying its teachings to denominational controversies and the dogmas of science.

On Tuesday, August 3, "Doctor Bob" (as he was affectionately known) spoke on the epistle's affirmation of human dignity, "Thou madest him a little lower than the angels." The text flew in the face of news from the western front. "Man's place in the universe is . . . too high for God to let brute force triumph in the world. . . . If the doctrines of Nietzsche are to prevail . . . man had better step down and yield his place to the lion or the whale or the diplodocus." Drunkenness too was brutalizing, just like Darwinism, and Doctor Bob touched on temperance as God's ideal. "Man can be the noblest thing in creation, or he can be worse than any lion or diplodocus: and woman can be a little better or a little worse than man."[2]

91

This was Lady Hope's cue. She now played her part in livening up the conference, secure in the knowledge that she was the sole representative of English evangelicalism in attendance. The next day, when she was to conduct the devotions at a temperance meeting, she spoke to Robertson after his class, introducing herself as "a friend of Charles Darwin." Or so Robertson wrote in a letter that afternoon. "She says that the great scientist was a Christian and was very fond of the Epistle to the Hebrews on which I am lecturing." Lady Hope also told her story at a morning prayer service, and Robertson repeated it from the platform. The editor of the nation's leading Baptist magazine, the *Watchman-Examiner*, was covering the conference. He insisted that Lady Hope write the story out so he could give it "the widest publicity." "It will give the world a new view of Charles Darwin," he declared.[3]

A fortnight later, the *Watchman-Examiner* carried Lady Hope's story under the title, "Darwin and Christianity."

It was on one of those glorious autumn afternoons, that we sometimes enjoy in England, when I was asked to go in and sit with the well known Professor, Charles Darwin. He was almost bedridden for some months before he died. I used to feel when I saw him that his fine presence would make a grand picture for our Royal Academy; but never did I think so more strongly than on this particular occasion.

He was sitting up in bed, wearing a soft embroidered dressing gown, of rather a rich purple shade. Propped up by pillows, he was gazing out on a far-stretching scene of woods and cornfields, which glowed in the light of one of those marvelous sunsets which are the beauty of Kent and Surrey. His noble forehead and fine features seemed to be lit up with pleasure as I entered the room.

He waved his hand toward the window as he pointed out the scene beyond, while in the other hand he held an open Bible, which he was always studying.

"What are you reading now?" I asked, as I seated myself by his bedside.

"Hebrews!" he answered—"still Hebrews. 'The Royal Book,' I call it. Isn't it grand?"

Then, placing his finger on certain passages, he commented on them.

I made some allusion to the strong opinions expressed by many persons on the history of the Creation, its grandeur, and then their treatment of the earlier chapters of the Book of Genesis.

He seemed greatly distressed, his fingers twitched nervously, and a look of agony came over his face as he said:

"I was a young man with unformed ideas. I threw out queries, suggestions, wondering all the time over everything; and to my astonishment the ideas took like wildfire. People made a religion of them."

Then he paused, and after a few more sentences on "the holiness of God" and "the grandeur of this Book," looking at the Bible which he was holding tenderly all the time, he suddenly said:

"I have a summer house in the garden, which holds about thirty people. It is over there," pointing through the open window. "I want you very much to speak there. I know you read the Bible in the villages. To-morrow afternoon I should like the servants on the place, some tenants and a few of the neighbors to gather there. Will you speak to them?"

"What shall I speak about?" I asked.

"CHRIST JESUS!" he replied in a clear, emphatic voice, adding in a lower tone, "and his salvation. Is not that the best theme? And then I want you to sing some hymns with them. You lead on your small instrument, do you not?"

The wonderful look of brightness and animation on his face as he said this I shall never forget, for he added:

"If you take the meeting at three o'clock this window will be open, and you will know that I am joining in with the singing."

How I wished that I could have made a picture of the fine old man and his beautiful surroundings on that memorable day!

This amazing account bears all the hallmarks of Lady Hope's anecdotal imagination. Years of tract and novel writing had made her a skilled raconteur, able to summon up poignant scenes and conversations, and embroider them with sentimental spirituality. The distinction between fact and fancy in her writings was never well defined. In her dotage now, she was even less likely to be hard-headed about history. Disgraced in England, displaced in America, she had only a short time before her cancer proved fatal. With everything to gain, what better than to trade off her title, ingratiate herself with "impressionable" Americans, and launch an edifying myth? Robertson was an eminent New Testament scholar. Well, then, have "professor" Darwin reading the Book of Hebrews, "on which," as Robertson noted, "I am lecturing." Have Darwin call it "the Royal Book" and be sure to mention the Royal Academy. Anglophiles warm to touches like that.

Much in Lady Hope's story is certainly fictitious. Darwin was not "almost bedridden for some months before he died." He was not "always studying" the Bible, and he had no particular feeling for its "grandeur."[4] He would never have asked Lady Hope to speak to anyone about "CHRIST JESUS . . . and his salvation." The notion of him "joining in with the singing" of gospel hymns from his bedroom window is preposterous.

However, the story cannot be dismissed as pure invention either. It contains startling elements of authenticity. Darwin's upstairs bedroom did overlook a "far-stretching scene of woods and cornfields." The sunsets in that direction were so grand that the boys used to climb into the pigeon loft by the kitchen garden to watch them (Figs. 10–11). Darwin also habitually retired to his room at three in the afternoon, lay down, smoked a cigarette, and had Emma or Bessy read to him until he fell asleep. He wore a "long bright coloured dressing gown" that, like all his overclothes, was very dark "with a reddish brown or purple tint." And out of the bedroom window, about four hundred yards away at the end of his thinking path, the Sandwalk, there was indeed a summer-house, from which singing might possibly have been heard on a still and pleasant day. But it was tiny, far too small for "thirty people"(Fig.12). Decades later, Lady Hope's imagination seems to have conflated the hymn-singing of Fegan's orphans at Down House with the Bible-reading in the old schoolroom, and placed the proposed event in an unlikely corner of Darwin's property.[5]

Of course some of this inside information was scattered about the *Life and Letters* and in other publications that had appeared by 1915. The more intimate tidbits might have been winkled out of members of the Darwin household, such as Parslow or Mrs. Sales, both involved with Fegan's mission in the 1880s.[6] But why should Lady Hope have gone to the trouble of collecting all these details, committing them to an otherwise hazy memory, and concocting a story around them that is so modest, relatively speaking, in its claims? For the most striking thing about the story is what it does *not* purport to be: the story of a deathbed conversion.

Darwin does not appear on his deathbed: he is merely resting sometime in the autumn of 1881, about six months before he died. He does not renounce evolution: he is simply made to express concern (with fingers twitching nervously as they often did when he was lost in thought) over the fate of his youthful speculations—a characteristic concern, in fact.[7] Nor does he embrace Christianity: he is only made to speak in favor of a brand of evangelicalism that, as he told Fegan, had "done more for the village . . . than all our efforts for many years." Although Lady Hope may have taken this to mean that "the great scientist was a Christian," as Robertson reported her, the story she finally put in print does not claim anything of the sort.

And, what is more, she clung tenaciously to her story, supplying further details when asked. Why, if sensational self-aggrandizement was her aim, did she not offer her most convincing version in the first place?

As the Northfield conference drew to a close Lady Hope registered her attendance with a bold signature in a Moody family guest book. Then she set off to resume her temperance work. During the American phase of the War, after 1917, she served as secretary of a charitable organization, the Office Families Fund. She went to live on the West Coast, probably for her health, and there in 1919 made out her will.[8] In the Los Angeles area she became friendly with a circle of religious leaders who heard her tell her story on several occasions. Shortly afterwards, they signed an affidavit vouching for many of its details and testifying to their "perfect confidence" in her "sincerity and reliability."[9]

Also about this time, a biology professor from Wheaton College near Chicago wrote to Lady Hope, asking for the story in her own hand. He promised not to publicize it during her lifetime. In reply, she sent him the fullest version yet. (It appeared in print some twenty years later.)[10] In November 1921, just before sailing for England, Lady Hope ran into an old acquaintance of her late husband, Commissioner Frederick Booth-Tucker of the Salvation Army, who was in San Francisco to dedicate a divisional headquarters. When he asked for "the actual particulars of her meeting with Darwin," she repeated the story once more. The following March, Booth-Tucker affirmed its main points in a letter published, coincidentally, the day after Lady Hope died in a suburb of Sydney, Australia.[11] She never made it home but she stuck to her story to the end (Fig. 13).

Much of the later testimony to Lady Hope's story shows how credulous even educated people can be. Her purported conversation with Darwin becomes more elaborate with each telling: now he asks for Moody and Sankey's hymns to be sung, and the implicit claim in her first account—that more than one interview took place—grows into as many as four visits. But there is much convincing new detail as well. Lady Hope claims to have been conducting meetings in Downe village itself when she first met Darwin. She was staying with a "lady" who lived "very near" Down House, and she knew the "large gate" that opened onto its "carriage drive." Darwin himself asked her to call at "three P.M."

She went upstairs and found him in "a large room with a high ceiling" just off the "landing." He was lying on a "sofa" beside a "fine bay window." "Mrs. Darwin" was present also, at least part of the time. She showed "some little (polite) displeasure" when the intent of the visit became clear, and for that reason—as well as the opposition of "the sons"—the summer-house service was never held.

All this new information has the ring of truth about it. Darwin had an exaggerated respect for the titled. A "Lady" who had helped in the village, who ministered in the homes of the elderly and the ill, might well have received an invitation to call on him in the weeks after his brother Erasmus's death, when his own health was giving "much cause for uneasiness." At this time, after all, he welcomed other guests— Aveling, Büchner, and Brodie Innes—whose religious concerns he shared. Lady Hope had more status than any of these men. Indeed, she was a leading figure in the national temperance movement, with personal backing from Lord Shaftesbury. Both Charles and Emma shared her concern with drunkenness too. And Lady Hope had lately lost her husband, as Emma feared she soon would.[12]

Also Darwin did lie on a sofa, not in bed, for his daily siesta; his tall, spacious room was off the upstairs landing and its windows shared the imposing bay added in 1843 to all three stories on the west side of the house. Emma would most definitely have stayed with him if Lady Hope had been allowed privileged access to this inner sanctum. Propriety dictated as much. And regardless of Lady Hope's reputation as a devout temperance worker, or as Mr. Fegan's lieutenant, regardless of her recent bereavement, Emma would not have tolerated anything so intrusive as personal evangelizing.[13]

Francis Darwin, if he was present in the house, would have felt just as strongly. After 1915, indeed, whenever Lady Hope's published story came to his notice, or the family's, the reaction was fast and furious.

6

LEGENDS ALIVE

L ADY HOPE'S STORY MISREPRESENTED DARWIN'S RELIGIOUS
views to a vastly greater extent than the family did in
the *Life and Letters*. But the distortion was one of degree, not kind. Both accounts were historically based; each
was adapted to a different audience. They contained the
stuff of legends.

Just as the *Life and Letters* was tailored for a liberal British
intelligentsia that placed a premium on religious moderation,
so Lady Hope pitched her story to a conservative American
populace for whom, increasingly, fervid commitment to the
Bible had become the test of religious orthodoxy. "Fundamentalists," they were called. The word was coined ap-
provingly in 1920 by the same editor in the same magazine
that reported her remarks at Northfield.[1] Most Fundamentalists had neither the inclination nor the interest to digest a
three-volume scientific biography. Their staple fare was low-
brow religious magazines, like the *Watchman-Examiner*.
When these papers began to circulate Lady Hope's story, the
most powerful Darwin legend ever was launched.

The story swept through the magazines like wildfire—not
only *Baptist World* (1915), *Bible Numerics* (1916), *Bible
Champion* (1924), and *Christian Fundamentalist* (1927) in
North America, but even British titles, *Honour* (1917), *The
Christian* (1922), *Life of Faith* (1925), and *Joyful News*
(1928). This storm of publicity coincided with the first anti-
evolution crusade in the United States and the last fling of

99

William Jennings Bryan at the Dayton, Tennessee "monkey trial" of 1925. Shrewdly, Bryan refused to exploit Lady Hope's story: he did not believe it showed a "positive change of view." But this did not deter other Fundamentalists, who lacked his lawyer's judgment.[2] Inflammatory tracts began to appear, with titles such as "Darwin on His Deathbed," "Darwin's Last Hours," "Darwin, 'The Believer,'" and "Darwin Returned to the Bible" (Fig. 14). These achieved an enormous circulation. Everywhere across Fundamentalist America, and to some extent in the nether regions of British evangelicalism, the conviction grew that Darwin had seen the light and died a penitent.

Rarely did anyone bother to check any of this with members of the Darwin family. When contacted, they of course denied Lady Hope's story vehemently. Francis labeled it "a work of imagination" (1915), a "fabrication" (1917), and "quite untrue" (1918). Referring inquirers to the *Life and Letters*, he insisted that Darwin died an agnostic. Henrietta, still more adamant, declared in 1922 that she herself was "present at his deathbed" and recorded his "last words," whereas Lady Hope was "not present during his last illness, or any illness." "He never recanted any of his scientific views. . . . The whole story has no foundation whatever." Leonard, Darwin's last surviving child, also homed-in on "the scene at his death-bed." He dismissed Lady Hope's account as a "hallucination" (1930) and "purely fictitious" (1934). The grandchildren passed on the family line with equal force. Lady Hope had given rise to an "absurd fiction" and a "lie" (1928). Darwin's deathbed conversion was a "myth" (1958).[3]

Such reactions were understandable. The family had every right to feel aggrieved at the way Lady Hope's story was exploited. And the story itself was justly repugnant to them, a weird confection of the plausible and the preposterous, though convincing enough to damage Darwin's public image. But what the family denied, angrily and repeatedly, was not simply Lady Hope's version of events; it was the

legend her story had started, the legend of a deathbed conversion. In refuting this—by reference to "last words," the
bedside "scene," and the *Life and Letters*—the family did
not offer historical arguments. They merely promoted their
own sanitized portrait of Darwin while neglecting the actual purport of Lady Hope's story and its authentic details
of time and place. They were too complacent. From the start,
they allowed Fundamentalists to set the terms of the debate.

Why? One reason is surely that the family failed to grasp
the long-term problem of protecting "Darwin." In Britain
he had remained in their safe custody, at least during Emma's
lifetime. The *Life and Letters* had insured this by warding
off militants like Aveling and Haeckel, who tried to hijack
him. But by the 1920s the family's "Darwin" had escaped
into the wider culture, and nowhere more strikingly than in
the United States. Here his name was linked to all sorts of
religious and political movements, often through the very
words of the *Life and Letters*. Communism, socialism, mod-
ernism, racism—the list was long even before Fundamentalism was added.

Now the family could not hope to rescue "Darwin," except perhaps by releasing fresh evidence to back up their
claim to know him best. But this was impossible in many
cases, and deemed imprudent in Lady Hope's. Arguing with
her in public would have suggested that she should be taken
seriously, which the incensed family naturally refused to do.
Anyway her "conversion" story was a rude import, "we
think . . . fabricated in [the] U.S.A.," as Henrietta wrote curtly.
It did not merit much attention, certainly no more than a
summary denial and a nod toward the official biography.[4]
This then became the family policy, with inevitable results:
legends collided, producing more historical heat than light.

Another reason why the Darwins never got past deny-
ing the Fundamentalist legend is that they were devoted to
their own. The legends embodied rival religious interests.
"With the Darwin family," an old Fundamentalist declared,

"the writer has no controversy whatever; but he has a great controversy with what they . . . represent": the arrogance of the "'Scientific' spirit."[5] To him the witness of Darwin himself was preferable to the family's because, in Lady Hope's story, he displayed that spirit duly penitent. Similarly, the Darwin family invested heavily in its own modest legend because certain members had a "great controversy" with what Fundamentalists stood for. They preferred the Darwin of the *Life and Letters*, not just because they had known him to be a temperate, respectable agnostic, but because the *Origin of Species* was a scientific refutation of fiat creationism.

The family members in question were of course the sons—evolutionists and freethinkers all. George died in 1912 and William in 1914, so neither of them heard of Lady Hope's story. Horace lived until 1928 but deferred to Francis and Leonard in debate. Francis, editor of the *Life and Letters*, tackled Lady Hope at least five times and once publicly accused her of falsehood. He also probably wrote the "very angry letter" that, it was said, "distrest her very much" and made her stop publishing her story.[6] Leonard pitched in too, and when Francis died in 1925, followed by Henrietta in 1927 and Bessy in 1928, he himself became a living legend, the last surviving child of Charles and Emma (Fig. 15).

Leonard's accession to the family headship opened a new phase of the *Life and Letters* legend, just as the first flurry of interest in the Fundamentalist legend was passing. Now the family's "Darwin" would be enshrined.

Leonard had been a maverick all his life. Born in 1850, he did not attend Cambridge like his brothers, nor did he follow them into banking, business, or science. Instead he spent twenty years in the army, then threw himself into civic controversy. In 1907 he became the first president of the Eugenics Society, an elite pressure group devoted to breeding better people. For decades he was its "leading spirit," arguing for legal and tax incentives to prevent "racial deterioration" in Britain. "All men in well-paid, honourable employments" should be able to have at least "four children," he believed, whereas the poor should be deterred from reproducing. With such policies the nation would stand proud in the "upward march" of evolution.[7]

Here Leonard was echoing his father's *Descent of Man*. His concern to legislate the "survival of the fittest" was shared by a scientific friend, the anthropologist and probable Piltdown hoaxer Arthur Keith. Or rather Keith, a dyed-in-the-wool Darwinian, was preoccupied with the corollary, eliminating the least fit, or "undesirables," from the nation's "stock." He could spot them by the size and shape of their skulls, in the same way he identified the Darwin males as fit members of the "landed and professional" middle class. Such men, who inherit and pass on capital, he argued, provide "the nests in which inventive genius may brood," just as the "highest forms" of animal life—placental mammals—nourish their young from the "floating capital of the mother's body."[8]

Darwin was Keith's "inventive genius" par excellence, a wonder-working figure whose touch had transformed the concept of human nature. On February 12, 1921, Darwin's birth date and fifty years to the month after the publication of the *Descent of Man*, Keith made a solemn pilgrimage to Down House, bearing a letter of introduction from Leonard. The house was still in the family but leased as a private school for young ladies. Keith wandered the grounds, marveling that here "Darwin, singlehanded, wrought the miracle of the nineteenth century. . . . He conquered the indulgences and temptations which beset inherited wealth, and . . . gave the world an untold fortune of knowledge in return for a limited allowance of capital and leisure."

Darwin's achievement to Keith was "a crowning example to justify our capitalistic system," and in a moving article he pleaded that Down House should be preserved for the nation:

Since my visit the property has been in the market, with what
result I have not learned. What if the owner now is one who
knows not Darwin, and is all unconscious that he has become the absolute owner of the Nazareth of Evolution? Is
it not right that this pulpit from which Darwin spoke to all
the world should become the home of a national Darwinian experimental garden?

The scheme needed the Darwins' backing. Keith roped in
Leonard, having him approve the article and draw up a
large-scale plan of the house and grounds.[9]

The article came out in *The R.P.A. Annual for 1923*—the
"R.P.A." being the Rationalist Press Association, a subscription book club founded by C. A. Watts. Watts went into
publishing in the 1880s and soon became the most success-
ful anti-Christian propagandist of his generation. Shunning
Bradlaugh's militant atheism, he aimed his list at the broad
church of unbelief: respectable Secularists and middle-class
freethinkers who preferred to call themselves "agnostics."
The literature was cheap but authoritative, with a strong
emphasis on evolution. In 1903 Watts slashed the price of
the *Origin of Species* in half with a six-penny paperbound
edition. It sold by the thousand for twenty years, with ad-
vertisements at the back for other "R.P.A. cheap reprints"
by Darwin's fiery followers, Haeckel and Büchner. Watts
also brought out a biography of Darwin in 1921, the year
Keith visited Down House. Its author, too, recalled Darwin's
"home life," and even included an anecdote from Leonard.[10]

Keith—Sir Arthur Keith now—was an honorary associate of the RPA, Leonard a fellow-traveler. They often met
to discuss the "eugenical control" of evolution and the fate
of Down House, which was "empty and rapidly deteriorating." Perhaps Leonard also spoke reverentially of his father, for Sir Arthur's devotion to Darwin was rising. In a
1925 lecture to freethinkers, *The Religion of a Darwinist*,
Sir Arthur uttered an impassioned credo. He urged his fel-

lows to read Darwin's books and "find that he who had studied Nature in all her moods gives utterance to only the gentlest of judgments, the most temperate of reasonings. Never did a man search more steadfastly or more whole-heartedly after truth in the realms of Nature, and yet he had nothing harsh to say, nothing against which he rebelled."[11] No scientist was ever so gifted, nor saint blessed.

Down House was still unsold in 1927 when Sir Arthur became president of the British Association for the Advancement of Science. He used his official address at the Association's annual gathering to inform the nation—live, via the BBC—that "Darwin's outline of man's history" was not just "impregnable" at present; "nay, . . . I am convinced that it never can be shaken." Afterwards, still at the podium, Sir Arthur renewed his plea for the preservation of Down House. The press picked it up, and the next morning a telegram came from George Buckston Browne, who had read Keith's remarks in *The Times*.

Buckston Browne, aged seventy-seven, was a "lonely and very rich" London urologist. Without sons to inherit his fortune, he offered to purchase Down House for the nation, restore its Victorian splendor, and endow the estate. Late in 1927 this was happily agreed in meetings with Sir Arthur and Leonard, who relayed the news to his family. He had heard how Buckston Browne worshiped Darwin from afar, ever since seeing him once as a student. Darwin altered the whole world's "current of thought" and so was "proportionately great," the doctor had enthused. "He believes," Leonard continued, "that in the future Downe will become a Mecca for the scientific world and his aim is to make it a worthy Mecca. . . . I feel strongly that we should give all the help we can."[12]

The family agreed, though time was short. Henrietta, Bessy, and Horace were to die within a year, leaving Leonard to gather family "relics" for the restoration. Also Sir Arthur's critics were rumbling ominously. The press had

played up his soulless Darwinian creed and now Fundamentalists filled his mailbox. Or "Daytonians," as he called
them, referring to the Tennessee yokels at the recent "monkey trial." "For such men and women all modern science
is rank heresy; they would gladly scrap Darwin and all his
works"—a frightful prospect. Watts and the RPA came to
the rescue by reprinting Sir Arthur's first plea for Down
House, his presidential address, and several other articles
in a pair of seven-penny paperbacks. In October 1928
Leonard's *What Is Eugenics?* came out in the same series,
appealing to "religion"—Sir Arthur's, not the Daytonians'—for the "motive force needed in the long struggle for
human progress which lies before us."[13]

At the end of the year Buckston Browne finally took possession of Down House. Renovations began immediately,
and gradually the interior was made to look like it had during Darwin's lifetime. The family treasures resumed their
old places, Emma's drawing-room grand piano came back
from the Church of Humanity (where Positivists had played
it since her death), and Buckston Browne had a white fox
terrier stuffed and placed in a basket in Darwin's study. It
was "Polly" of course, returned to haunt the house after half
a century. Leonard kept an eye on the decorations and Buckston Browne spared no expense.[14] Six months—and over
£30,000—later Down House was opened to the public.

A marquee stood on the lawn and the garden was gay
with flags on Friday, June 7, 1929, as hundreds of guests arrived, eager to catch a glimpse of the legendary Leonard.
Buckston Browne, addressing the crowd from the verandah,
formally transferred the property to the care of the British
Association. Then Sir Arthur came forward and took his
friend's place, just beneath Darwin's bedroom window, from
where Lady Hope had described "a far-stretching scene of
woods and cornfields" (Fig.16).

Before him, ranged against this rural backdrop, were leading scientists, foreign dignitaries, second- and third-gener-

ation Darwins and their children. It was a select audience, bourgeois and well-bred, gracing a green and pleasant land. Sir Arthur struck up a fitting theme, paying tribute to the "great man" who "came of a stock which has lived for more than 3,000 years on English soil."

> Down House was an abode of goodness as well as of genius. . . . In the place where we are now met, in these grounds, gardens, orchards, meadows, and walks, and within these walls, were slowly hammered hot from fact new doctrines which, radiating out from here, slowly penetrated to the ends of the earth, giving humanity a new interpretation of living things and of its relationship to them. Human thought was forcibly and permanently thrust from its old time-honoured ruts.

Slyly, Sir Arthur pitched his speech to the RPA members present. Darwin, he declared, "permitted the bare, unhusked truth to speak for itself; he went only so far as the light of reason would carry him. Only men who teach thus continue to teach for all time. Down House, then, is . . . a common heritage for truthseekers of all countries and of all centuries, . . . a permanent sanctuary for Darwinian pilgrims."[15]

Watts crowned the ceremony for the RPA by publishing Sir Arthur's speech and reissuing the *Origin of Species* and the *Descent of Man* in its new "Thinker's Library," which sold one hundred thousand copies that year. The reprint idea was Leonard's. In 1929 the Library also first carried a fifty-four-page booklet entitled *Autobiography of Charles Darwin*. This was the *Life and Letters* text, cheaply repackaged, and the sales were phenomenal—six huge editions in twenty years. Leonard still had qualms about it. "My father's autobiography . . . certainly was not written with the view to publication," he warned; "the expressions he used were not selected with that care which he would have exercised if he had thought that there was the slightest chance of its being subject to carping criticism."

But no abuse was heard, no damage done. Under Watts, the family's "Darwin" enjoyed a fitting, agnostic imprint, just as—thanks to Sir Arthur—his home had become a rationalist shrine. In Watts's guidebook, *London for Heretics,* Down House was even listed among Ethical Societies, Unitarian chapels, and the Church of Humanity as a site for Sunday excursions.[16]

Buckston Browne, his dream realized, now gained a new lease on life and continued to look after the estate for fifteen years. "I assure you that at Down House we frequently have charabancs laden with tourists," he chortled at the 1931 RPA annual dinner, "and some of the tourists will not come in," even though "no one exceeded Darwin in reverence." Leonard, too, got his second (or third) wind. He grew a beard at the age of eighty-four and looked remarkably like his father—so much so that Sir Arthur recorded his cranial measurements for posterity. The same year Leonard tackled the deathbed legend once more, in the correspondence columns of *The Times.* His denial was twice reprinted in Watts's *Literary Guide and Rationalist Review,* which bemoaned the "output of myths about the great."[17]

Leonard died in 1943 but, despite his efforts, the deathbed legend lived on, circulating as vigorously as the family's in the cheap *Autobiography.* By coincidence Lady Hope's story surfaced in the Edinburgh daily, *The Scotsman,* in May 1958, just weeks after Darwin's grand-daughter Nora Barlow published, at long last, the full text of the autobiography, "with original omissions restored." Nora recalled the family's "hot feelings" about the religious section, and the children's "divided loyalties," but herself saw the contested passages as "revealing flashes lighting up the past." She saw nothing of the sort in the *Scotsman* story, or rather the deathbed legend she took it for. It "has no foundation whatever," she chided the editor, quoting in full her aunt Henrietta's denial.[18]

Nora's riposte came just in time to get top billing in the Darwin centenary number of the RPA's magazine, *The Hu-*

manist (Fig.17). "The Myth of Darwin's Conversion," howled the headline, which was followed by a rather calmer story, "Darwin of Downe," featuring the autobiography's "damnable" passage. This, however, was the last time British unbelievers would dismiss the deathbed legend. Just as the family's legend had been laid to rest by Nora Barlow, so now it was the Fundamentalists' turn. In 1960 and 1965 *The Humanist* published a pair of "devastating" articles by Pat Sloan in which, for the first time, Lady Hope was taken seriously as a historical witness. Sloan failed to discover her identity— she remained "shadowy" and a "mystery"—but he did muster evidence "sufficient to deflate" the deathbed legend and "reduce it to a merely civil reception by the invalid Darwin to a visiting lady evangelist," perhaps a "collaborator of Fegan." "Despite the Darwins' doubts," he insisted, "Lady Hope may at some time have visited" Down House.[19]

The irony of this disclosure was doubly rich. For not only was it the RPA that published Sloan's hard-won evidence— evidence that embarrassed the freethinking Darwins' denials; it was also an unbeliever who did the historical spadework—spadework that might have been performed by those who stood to profit religiously from it. But "the children of this world are in their generation wiser than the children of light," as the recent history of Lady Hope's story makes clear. Decades after Sloan's articles came out, the deathbed legend still flourishes in evangelical books, tracts, and magazines— and even occasionally on television. It is an ironic, backhanded compliment to Darwin that those who revile his theories continue to attach such significance to his religious judgment.

Of course some evangelicals, overzealous for truth, have rushed to refute Lady Hope's story. It has spawned a minor cottage-industry among North American neo-creationists, who argue that their cause is "not served by spurious reporting, nor by the dissemination of unfounded accounts." But this, too, is deeply ironic: creationist tilts at "Darwin's last hours" and the "conversion story" read like the Darwin family's own propaganda—although recent research has at last identified Lady Hope.

Even so, no one to date—in North America—has exploited Sloan's articles. They are cited prominently in the standard work on Down House, now over twenty years old, but their existence has been ignored. Only a British creationist has used, or rather abused, the articles in a regrettable study of Darwin's religious life. Accusing Sloan of joining a "deliberate conspiracy" to obscure Lady Hope, the author concludes "confidently" that she "did visit Darwin shortly before his death" and hear him profess "renewed faith in the Christian Gospel."[20]

By now the pattern is tiresomely familiar. Neo-creationists are only the latest group to way-lay Darwin. Everyone has tried to get, or keep, him on their side—Fundamentalists, scientists, Secularists, Lady Hope, and the family alike. In the long run, none of them has succeeded. They have all been upstaged. Darwin has turned out to be bigger, more complex, more awkwardly historical than anyone imagined. He especially resists latter-day Procrusteans who would force him into conformity with their views.

Born to wealth, reared in privilege, advantaged by traveling the globe as a young man, Charles Darwin came to view life in a way that, he believed, would cost him dear if people knew his innermost thoughts. As an evolutionist in the turbulent, half-reformed, Anglican-dominated society of young Victoria's reign, he devised schemes for concealment, "fortifications for the self."[21] His existence became contradictory, his life a camouflage. He became profoundly ill. Outwardly liberal and polite, of modest opinions, the pillar of the parish, he was inwardly Darwin *contra mundum*, the failed ordinand, the Christian manqué, the angry unbeliever. He weathered the storm of self-exposure in the *Origin of Species* and the *Descent of Man*, but even in late Victorian times, with fame and fortune secure, he waited ten years after the word was coined before calling himself an agnostic. And still he shrank from controversy, from atheistic alliances, from the taint of irreligion. For Emma's sake, and the family's, Charles was determined to be his own man.

Perhaps the time has come to let him be.

APPENDIX A

SOURCES OF THE LEGEND, 1882–1958

ERE FOLLOW THE COMPLETE TEXTS OF EVERY KNOWN
original report or recollection that has contributed
to the deathbed legend. Only Lady Hope's 1915
Watchman-Examiner story, given verbatim in chapter 5, is
omitted. Full references are provided in the bibliography.

The Tenby Tale, 1882

In May 1882, a week after Darwin's burial in Westminster Abbey, Dearman Birchall (1828–97), a Leeds merchant-turned-Gloucestershire squire, went with his wife and their four children for a holiday in the south Wales resort of Tenby. On the first Sunday he heard "Mr Huntingdon" preach an astonishing sermon, recalled in the diary entry below. Tenby had been the home of Emma Darwin's Allen aunts; the Darwins' first cousin, Rev. John Allen Wedgwood, still lived there. He had officiated at their marriage in 1839 and conducted the funeral of Charles' brother Erasmus on September 1, 1881.[1] Perhaps clerical chit-chat between Wedgwood and Huntingdon got worked into the sermon.

May 7. We are perfectly charmed with the large old parish church, its services and clergyman Mr Huntingdon, who is almost inspired it seemed to us. In the morning he preached

113

on the text "In my Father's house are many mansions"; in the evening, "This is life eternal to know the only true God and Jesus Christ whom thou has sent." He spoke of Darwin one of the greatest thinkers who had in his last utterances confessed his true faith. His eloquence amazed and delighted us.

Source: VEREY, ED., *DIARY OF A VICTORIAN SQUIRE* (1983), P. 137

The Eadie Note, 1885

A few months after the Tenby sermon, Thomas Cooper (1805–92) obtained the second legendary report. He was not uncritical, having himself been a working-class radical and freethinker for many years. Infidel conversion stories had been the stock-in-trade of his religious opponents. But he was now a Christian, baptized in 1859 as the *Origin of Species* was going to press. He stumped the country defending the faith to unchurched workers, and in 1885 he first gave them the news of Darwin's conversion. It came from the nephew of the late Rev. John Eadie, for thirty-three years professor of biblical literature in the United Secession Divinity Hall, Glasgow. Eadie died on June 3, 1876, so the confessional letter that, his nephew alleged, he had received from Darwin dated from the period before Darwin called himself an agnostic (though he had long since finished with Christianity).[2] No letters to or from Eadie are preserved in the Darwin Archive.

Now, notwithstanding all these bold sceptical declarations of persons who shared Charles Darwin's views, it is by no means clear as to what were his real religious views, or what changes they underwent. I hold in my hand a small note which will set some of you a-thinking. I was lecturing at

Beverley, in Yorkshire, two years and a half ago, when this note was sent to me.

The Vicarage, Beverley:
Tuesday, Sept. 19th, 1882.

My Dear Sir,—

I heard your lecture last night with pleasure; and I beg to inform you that, five weeks ago, I sent a letter to Mr. Darwin's son, addressed to my uncle, the late Professor Eadie, from his father,—in which he says that he can with confidence look to Calvary.

Wishing you great success in your lectures here,

I remain yours respectfully,
Robert Eadie, F.R.G.S.

Thos. Cooper, Esq.

I do not know when Charles Darwin told Professor Eadie that he "could with confidence look to Calvary"—or what he really meant by it. We were told some time ago that young Mr. Darwin is now trying to collect his father's letters, that he may publish them. Of course, he will insert the letter to the late Professor Eadie. Let us hope we shall have some explanation of it.

Source: COOPER, THOUGHTS AT FOURSCORE
AND EARLIER (1885), PP. 138–39

The Toronto Sermon, 1887

A journalist with the Toronto *Mail*, Charles Dedûchson, was on to a hot story when he sent Thomas Huxley a report of a sermon by a local evangelical parson, Rev. John Mutch (1852–97) of Chalmers Presbyterian Church.[3] Huxley, after consulting Francis Darwin (App. C), poured cold water on the report, but the mystery remains: why would an earnest young M.A. of the University of Toronto, only three years in his first charge, preaching to a large and literate suburban congregation, utter anything like Deduchson's words? On what conceivable authority could Mutch have claimed that Darwin converted on his deathbed?[4]

Assuming that Deduchson himself was not lying, any of three channels might have connected Mutch with Lady Hope. (1) He was related to the Scottish evangelist James J. Scroggie, who had worked closely with D. L. Moody in his 1881–84 British mission. Lady Hope was also involved.[5] (2) Fegan visited Toronto twice in 1884, and afterwards annually, bringing scores of his orphan boys to start new lives in Canada. Despite his later testimony (App. D), he may have imported news about Darwin dating from the period of his Downe mission—news that, badly distorted, finally reached Mutch.[6] (3) At least two University of Toronto students attended Moody's 1886 college "summer school for Bible study" at Mount Hermon, Massachusetts, near the Moody home in East Northfield. They may have picked up rumors about Darwin circulating in the Moody family, then, back in Toronto that autumn, passed on the gossip to student members of the Chalmers congregation, who informed their minister.[7]

A far simpler explanation is that Mutch contrived the sermon anecdote as a preemptive strike against Darwin's famous colleague, Alfred Russel Wallace, who was to lecture on evolution at the University of Toronto a few weeks later.[8]

Office of The Mail, Editorial Department
Toronto, January 24th, 1887

Sir,

Will you pardon me if I ask you a question which I believe you are specially qualified to answer?

Rev. Mr Mutch, a Presbyterian clergyman of this city, recently preaching on the inspiration of the Bible, denounced

modern science and said Mr Darwin, when on his death-
bed, abjectly whined for a minister and renouncing Evolu-
tion, sought safety in the blood of the Saviour. Is there any
truth in this?

So far away from the intellectual centres it is hard to keep
en raport [sic] with scientific truths and as an humble though
distant admirer of your writings, I ask pardon for thus trou-
bling you.

I beg to remain,
Yours obediently,
[signed] Chas Dedûchson

Thomas H. Huxley Esq, F.R.S.
London

Feby 12. 1887

Sir

I have the best authority for informing you that the state-
ment which you attribute to the Revd Mr. Mutch of Toronto
that "Mr Darwin, when on his death bed, abjectly whined
for a minister and renouncing Evolution, sought safety in
the blood of the Saviour" is totally false and without any
kind of foundation.

You are at liberty to use this letter as you think fit—though
I can hardly imagine that even reverend fabricators or pro-
mulgators of lies about the dead can be worth the notice of
honest men.

I am
Yours truly
[signed] T. H. Huxley

Source: HUXLEY PAPERS, 8:136–37, 138–39

Sir Robert's Evidence, 1907

The best evidence to date that Lady Hope, while living in England between 1881 and 1913, did *not* stay silent about her encounter with Darwin (cf. App. D) is contained in a footnote to an anti-evolutionary book by Sir Robert Anderson (1841–1918). Sir Robert, a Dublin barrister, was an expert on "political crime"; he joined the Home Office in the 1860s to help combat the Irish Republican Brotherhood. In 1888, during the "Jack the Ripper" murders, he was appointed London's Assistant Commissioner of Metropolitan Police and head of the Criminal Investigation Department at Scotland Yard, where he remained until 1901.

During this period Sir Robert became one of the capital's best-connected and most influential evangelical leaders. "A controversialist by temperament, with the incisive categorical habit of the legal mind," he tackled religious crimes and heresies in numerous books, lectured and preached prolifically, and even assisted with village missions. Fegan, a fellow Plymouth Brother, was a sometime co-evangelist and one of his oldest friends; they met during Moody's first British campaign in 1873–75. Only illness prevented Fegan from honoring Sir Robert's request to write his biography. Another warm friend was Lady Hope.[9] In 1907 London's top detective vouched for her veracity in these words:

I may add that a friend of mine who was much with Darwin during his last illness assures me that he expressed the greatest reverence for the Scriptures and bore testimony to their value.

Source: ANDERSON, *IN DEFENCE: A PLEA FOR THE FAITH* (1907), P. 95N

Doctor Bob's Report, 1915

The first person in North America to hear about Darwin from Lady Hope herself was probably A. T. Robertson (1863–1934), professor of New Testament interpretation at Southern Baptist Theological Seminary, Louisville, and author of the monumental *Grammar of the Greek New Testament in the Light of Historical Research* (1914). By 1915 Robertson had become an institution at the annual summer schools organized by William R. Moody, the evangelist's son, at East Northfield, Massachusetts. That year "Doctor Bob" gave fifteen expositions of the Epistle to the Hebrews at the General Conference of Christian Workers, held from July 30 to August 15.[10]

In the audience to hear his fourth talk, "God's Ideal for Man," was Lady Hope. She was to lead the devotions in a "gospel temperance" meeting the next day, and as Doctor Bob—a prohibitionist—had touched on teetotalism from the platform, she had good cause to approach him then. But her main pretext lay in his remarks on human dignity ("a little lower than the angels," according to Heb. 2:7) and the degrading doctrine of evolution. "Atheistic evolution," that is. Unknown to his noble interlocutor, Doctor Bob was quite "willing to believe" in evolution with "'God' at the top." "I can stand it if monkeys can," he would twit his seminarians.[11] What Lady Hope had heard, however, was an implicit slur on Darwin, and she sought to set the record straight.

That afternoon Doctor Bob summed up their conversation in the letter to his son Archibald extracted below. He repeated Lady Hope's story from the Northfield platform, probably the next day, and perhaps obtained its publication a few weeks later in the Louisville-based *Baptist World*.[12] Time and again in subsequent months he was asked whether he stood by the story. This proved an em-

barrassment to his skills as a textual critic. Finally, after
hearing from the Darwin family, Doctor Bob denied spon-
sorship entirely (App. C). In a 1926 article on "science and
the future life" he mentioned Darwin as one whose religious life had become so "atrophied" that in the end he was
"unable to feel any response to the call for the worship of
God[,] if there even was a God at all[,] of which he had
grave doubts."[13]

The Northfield
East Northfield, Mass.
Aug. 4, '15
5 P.M.

My darling Archibald:
    *. . . I send a paper about my lectures. I hope you can all
come here some day. I am kept very busy, but I enjoy it. I
meet a great many pleasant people. Some Quakers, Leeds,
of Philadelphia, are taking me to the auditorium every morning in their machine. This morning Lady Hope, of England,
a friend of Charles Darwin, came up to tell me of her pleasure in my lectures. She says that the great scientist was a
Christian and was very fond of the Epistle to the Hebrews
on which I am lecturing. . . .*

Source: A. T. ROBERTSON CORRESPONDENCE

Booth-Tucker's Testimony, 1922

Lady Hope, with her second husband T. A. Denny, was
a loyal friend of the Salvation Army. When the son-in-law
of its head, General William Booth, visited San Francisco
to open a new divisional headquarters in early November
1921 he was no doubt pleasantly surprised to meet her.
Frederick   St.   George   de   Lautour   Booth-Tucker
(1853–1929), commander of the Army in India from 1906

to 1919, already knew of Lady Hope's interview with Darwin, possibly from the 1916 *Bombay Guardian* article. Now he wanted the "actual particulars" firsthand. What he heard was repeated from memory in the following letter to *The Christian*, sent in reply to Henrietta Darwin Litchfield (App. C). Nothing Lady Hope told him tempered his view of evolution, however. He wrote some months later that it was among those "foolish theories, impossible of proof," for which "men who invent" them are "exalted to be Professors in our Colleges and Theological Seminaries, while their books are heralded by the Press and Publishers as marvels of scientific wisdom. One of them is honoured with a place in Westminster Abbey."[14]

Dear Sir,—

With reference to the notice regarding Charles Darwin, in "The Christian" of Feb. 23, the actual facts are, I believe, as follows:—

Lady Hope was conducting meetings in the village shortly before Mr. Darwin's death. She visited him in his home, and he said that he was very pleased to hear about her meetings. She expressed surprise, seeing that she had always understood that he held contrary views. He replied that a great deal more had been made of some of his views than he had ever intended, and that there was nothing like the Gospel— or words to that effect. Turning to the Bible, which was open before him, he referred to the wonderful depth and beauty of the Epistle to the Hebrews from which he was then reading.

The above is, of course, quite different from the "highly coloured" story which Mrs. Litchfield contradicts. Lady Hope can hardly be held responsible for the embellishments of newspaper reporters, but one can scarcely believe that the facts as above stated can be pure fabrication. They seem rather to fit in with the character of Mr. Darwin as pictured in Mrs. Litchfield's own book.

It would perhaps be interesting to learn from Mrs. Litch-field whether her father did read and admire the Bible. The picture of the old scientist clinging to the Bible and its teach-ings during his last days, is certainly very interesting to those of us who believe in it as the Book of books, and one would like to know from his own daughter what she had to say upon this point.

I may add that the above particulars were given me by Lady Hope herself, a few weeks ago, when I happened to meet her in San Francisco, and asked her for the actual par-ticulars of her meeting with Darwin. I quote, however, from memory.—Yours, etc.,

F. B. Tucker
Salvation Army Headquarters
Queen Victoria-st., E.C. 4.

Source: TUCKER, THE CHRISTIAN, MAR. 9, 1922, P. 26

The Los Angeles Affidavit, 1922

In early 1922 William Jennings Bryan (1860–1925), Pres-byterian layman and three-times-defeated Democratic can-didate for the U.S. presidency, emerged as the front-runner in the Fundamentalist campaign to purge evolution from the nation's schools. The campaign died with him three years later but for the moment he looked invincible. His platform oratory, his notorious *New York Times* article, "God and Evolution," and his much touted offer to pay $100 to any professor who could reconcile evolution and the Bible made him the hero of voiceless citizens, resentful at the "scientific soviet" foisting Darwin on their young.[15]

Los Angeles was Fundamentalism's West Coast head-quarters. There Lyman and Milton Stewart of the Union Oil Company bankrolled the twelve pamphlets, *The Funda-mentals* (1910–15), which gave the movement its name.

They also founded the Bible Institute of Los Angeles, which in 1922 hosted the fourth annual convention of the World's Christian Fundamentals Association. Among the city's grassroots faithful were a handful of Lady Hope's friends who had heard her tell of meeting Darwin. Supposing that Bryan could capitalize on the story, they reconstructed it in a signed affidavit addressed to him, testifying to Lady Hope's "sincerity and reliability." The prime signatory was Melville Dozier (1846–1936), a former faculty member and vice-principal of the State Normal School at Los Angeles (now UCLA) and for six years assistant superintendent of the city's schools. He had worked with the plant breeder Luther Burbank, and still sometimes lectured on astronomy, so his authority was "scientific"—though he was nonetheless an upstanding member of the First Baptist Church.[16]

The affidavit was prepared by Mrs. Annette Parkinson Smith, not one of the signatories. It embellishes or deviates from Lady Hope's *Watchman-Examiner* story in several key respects: four visits to Down House are now mentioned; Mrs. Darwin and her sons are said to have scotched the summer-house service; and a "very angry letter" from the sons is blamed for distressing the noble lady, who had come to America "to overcome the grief of her husband's death."

Bryan was too bright to bite. He knew about the story and the Darwin family's denial. Without impugning Lady Hope, he replied that using it would only aid the other side in the fight against evolution. Darwin's own words, which he enclosed, were better ammunition. In fact, he himself had just sponsored them as "Darwin's Confession" in a new edition of his booklet *The Bible and Its Enemies*, published by Moody Bible Institute.[17]

Los Angeles, California
June 7th 1922

Honorable Mr. Bryan,

Respected Sir

Your published reply to teachers of evolution of man from monkeys &c,—of "the Chicago infidel foundry" (as Rev. Dr. Oliver calls Chicago University)—is real cause for satisfaction, to all who believe in the inspired Word of God. We thank you, Sir.

May I enquire if you know of Lady Hope's interviews with Prof. Darwin? not the notorious Lady Frances Hope, but the widow of Sir James Hope, Admiral in the British Naval Service, and she an earnest Christian worker all her life, and the originator of the famous "Coffee-house" System in England.

We have had the honor, and the pleasure, of her friendship while in Los Angeles, for two years or so,—and heard from her own lips, several times, the account of her visits to Dr. Darwin's home—at his request—and of her conversations with him.

Without delaying for your reply, Sir, may I give you briefly the story.—Dr. Darwin sent his request that she call upon him—he a semi-invalid—when she was visiting in his village in the south of England. He had to recline on his couch; and Lady Hope was surprised to note that he was reading the Bible. With customary English reticence, she did not remark about this on her first visit, but on her second visit he was again reading the Bible, and she said she "was rather surprised," "as that did not seem to accord with the theories usually ascribed to him."

"Oh"! he replied "those theories of evolution! Oh! I put out those theories when I was a young man, searching, searching for knowledge, and they made a religion of them! Oh! if I could only undo them"! and Dr. Darwin appeared much agitated as he said these words, evidently thinking that his hypotheses had done great harm. He expressed himself similarly on another occasion, so that Lady Hope was quite convinced he repudiated them.

Dr. Darwin had his Bible in his arm as she entered on another day, and showed her that he was reading the Epistle to the Hebrews, and he said "I call that the royal epistle."

He also said, "You see that summer-house (on the spacious lawn). I built it with my own hands. It holds 30 people, and I want you to hold gospel meetings in it, and call in the tenants and neighbors, and sing the attractive new gospel songs (Sankey's) so that I can hear them through the open window, as I recline on this couch." He was unable to go down himself.

But Mrs Darwin, and their sons, knowing that the fame of the family rested upon said evolution theories,—and, probably, as one remarked to me recently—the income from the sale of the books—did not care to welcome a visitor who brought a gospel message, and Mrs. D. showed some little (polite) displeasure when present in the room, and the gospel meeting was never held in the summer-house.

When Lady Hope was at Moody Institute, Chicago, a preacher or lecturer there referred to said Darwinian theories, at the close of the address she told the speaker of Mr. Darwins later views,—and the Moody Church published some account (with some variation) in their paper.[18] This came to the knowledge of Dr. D.'s sons, and they wrote her a "very angry letter," which distrest her very much. She had come to this country hoping to overcome the grief of her husband's death, and was in no condition to endure such an attack. So for that sole reason she avoided publishing the facts (in print), tho' she very much wished to do so. But was very willing to state said facts in private interviews, and did so on several occasions in my presence.

Prof. Melville Dozier, who has done eminent service on Board of Education, &c, for many years—listened to her account one Sunday afternoon shortly before she was to

*leave Los Angeles—when we had an impromptu sympo-
sium on Prayer, and the Holy Spirit's guidance in prayer—
with Prof. & Mrs. Warner present, and my two daughters (who attend California Bible College) and Lady H's
Secretary, Mr Reginald Chorlton who is himself a true
Christian gentleman, and gospel lecturer. (Travel, biography &c) Rev. Dr. Elwood Lyon (L.L.D., D.D.) and his
wife, Rev[.] Susie Lyon, came from Pasadena on another
occasion, purposely to hear this from herself, and she willingly told them, as above, and the same in the presence of
other persons also.*

*We all regret that, so far as we know now, Lady Hope—
who died a few weeks ago in Australia on her way to England—left no written statement on the subject.—we hope
to hear that she has, however. Let me say she was in her 80th
year, but had lectured 4 times in Australia, almost 6 weeks
before her death, and was in full possession of her really
splendid mental faculties. Now, as she has passed away, there
is no objection on behalf of her personal feelings, to publishing these facts.*

*Prof. Dozier, a Christian gentleman whom the Bible In-
stitute is pleased to honor as such, and as a scholar and a
scientist—will formulate some witness of said persons, to
having heard this from Lady Hope herself. Every effort is
needed to counteract teaching of unBiblical theories in L.A.
schools, High Schools, University, &c.*

*We have had occasion to see that evolutionist "scien-
tists" (many of them) really* hate *the name of God, and the
Bible.*

*"Nevertheless the foundation of God standeth sure." And
may God guide and bless you, Sir, in showing the truth
("plumb") & the unshakeable solidity of that foundation.
Pardon me—and thank you again.*

*I am, Honored Sir, Yours faithfully
(Mrs.) Annette Parkinson Smith.*

Los Angeles, Cal.
June 12th 1922

Hon. Wm Jennings Bryan,
Washington, D.C.

Dear Sir

We testify to the accuracy of the statements in the accompanying letter from Mrs. A. Smith to yourself as touching what was said by Lady Hope in our presence concerning the attitude of Prof. Darwin in the latter part of his life relative to his theory of evolution as published in his earlier life.

We also testify to our perfect confidence in the sincerity and reliability of Lady Hope, for whose life and character we entertain the most profound respect.

Respectfully,
[signed] Melville Dozier
[signed] Elwood P. Lyon, (Ph.D., D.D.)
[signed] Mrs Susie E. Lyon
[signed] H. R. Warner, A.M., Dept. Science,
California College
[signed] Mary B. Warner

William Jennings Bryan
Villa Serena
Miami, Florida
January 31, 1923

Mrs. Annette Parkman [sic] Smith,
Los Angeles, California.

My dear Madam:

Your favor at hand. My attention has been called several times to the statement made by Lady Hope. I read the statement and did not attach much importance to it for two reasons; first because I thought the language quoted did not show a positive change of view and, second, because a recantation just before his death would not undo the harm done by his books. I have never used the quotation because

I think it tends to weaken our case rather than to strengthen it. The question is not whether Darwin at the last moment came back to Christianity—as Christians we can believe this possible—but unless he specifically repudiated his views as to the origin of man it would simply strentghen [sic] the theistic evolutionists who, in my judgment, are more dangerous than the materialistic evolutionists because they claim to believe in God as Creator although they put Him so far away that He is likely to exert a decreasing influence over their lives. The atheist shocks us into resistance while the theistic evolutionist is more apt to mislead us.

Since I first read Lady Hope's interview, I have seen in an atheistic apper [sic] recently an editorial saying that the Darwin family had denied the truth of the Lady Hope interview. You will find in the enclosed address on "The Menace of Darwinism" a quotation from Darwin which shows how completely his hypothesis destroyed his own religious faith.

> *Appreciating your friendly interest, I am*
> *Very truly yours*
> *W. J. Bryan*
> *WJB:T*
>
> *Dictated by Mr. Bryan:*
> *Signed in his absence.*

Source: WILLIAM JENNINGS BRYAN PAPERS, GENERAL CORRESPONDENCE, 35

The Anglican Anecdote, 1928

As a young Russian intellectual Ivan Nikolayevitsh Panin (1855–1942) joined nihilist plots against the czar and was forced into exile. Eventually he gained admission to Harvard University, where he became vice-president of the Philosophical Club and graduated with honors in 1882. Among his Harvard philosopher-friends were William James and Ralph

Waldo Emerson, but for all their liberal influence Panin soon converted from agnosticism to Christianity. In 1890 his whole life was again "revolutionised" when he "discovered the phenomenal mathematical design" underlying the Greek text of the New Testament. Later he found that the Hebrew Old Testament had a similar structure, and he spent the next fifty years making cabbalistic calculations to restore the Scriptures' original, autograph texts. His findings were reported at intervals in the small magazine he edited, *Bible Numerics*.[19]

As the calculations dragged on, *Bible Numerics* turned into a magpie's diary, full of bright bits and pieces that Panin picked up from correspondents and the evangelical press. In 1916 he was among the first to reprint Lady Hope's account from the *Watchman-Examiner*. The story snowballed, and by 1928 he had enough material to pack two issues, headlined "Darwin on His Deathbed Again" and "Darwin Dies a Christian."

Panin was credulous, always begging questions. His "scientific" textual criticism was itself a mathematical mystification of Fundamentalist belief. Needless to say, he had no doubts about the *Bible Numerics* anecdote reprinted below. Enough for him that it came from an upright clergyman, though no evidence has been found to suggest that Darwin and Friedrich Max Müller, the Oxford professor of comparative philology, were ever more than occasional correspondents who disputed the origin of language.[20]

. . . An Anglican Rector, of the best standing, whose name, if needed, will presumably not be refused, writes to the editor:

"As to Darwin's Deathbed: Miss G. C. (full name in the original) of my congregation tells me that as a girl of twenty she once dined alone at Oxford with Professor Max Muller [sic &c]; the conversation turned on Evolution; and Max Muller told her that his great and intimate friend Charles Darwin had spoken somewhat in these terms to him: that after publishing the theory of Evolution he was very perplexed on its bearing on the Christian Religion; that he

turned to the Scriptures, and became a firm Christian; the
position is odd; as both his son and grandson would seem
to deny his Christianity."

Source: PANIN, *BIBLE NUMERICS*, SEPT.–OCT. 1928, PP. 4–5

Lady Hope's Last Words, 1940

Eighteen years in her grave, Lady Hope spoke again when
S. James Bole (1875–1956), professor of biology in New
John Fletcher College (a Holiness institution in Oskaloosa,
Iowa), published the following undated letter. Bole had received it from her in the early 1920s and promised to keep
it private during her lifetime. He was then a professor at
Wheaton College near Chicago—"the whole Biology Department," in fact—and perhaps the only early Fundamentalist with advanced training in the life sciences. In 1922 he
placed his pen at Bryan's disposal to help combat evolution.[21] Bryan encouraged him, and within a few months Bole
finished an anti-Darwinian manuscript featuring Lady
Hope's letter. She had died in March that year, so he was
free to publish. But Bryan urged caution, as he had before
(see above).

> You lay great emphasis upon Darwin's attitude at the close
> of his life, as related by Lady Hope, but ignore his own state-
> ment of his agnostic views entertained only a short time be-
> fore. I believe that we have much more to gain by using him
> against himself to show how his doctrine led him away from
> every Christian principle, than by emphasizing his return
> at the last moment. If we omit the proven effect of the doc-
> trine upon himself and quote only Lady Hope's report of
> his last hours Darwinites will be quick to use his last atti-
> tude as proof that Darwinism does not mislead Christians.
> Lady Hope's testimony does not indicate a recantation and
> it does not show any such attitude as would answer the in-

dictment made against him. If you use Lady Hope's testimony at all it ought to be after you have pointed out his wanderings and then show that his experience in the wilderness into which his doctrine led him, was so unsatisfactory that he had to come back in his dying moments to the consolation of the Christian's faith—adding that while he might be repentant and forgiven, he could not undo the wrong he had done or make amends for the injustice of which he had been guilty.[22]

Bole took the point. No reference to Lady Hope appears in his articles reprinted in 1926 as *The Modern Triangle*. Darwin, he claimed, "little by little . . . accepted the belief in an evolutionary philosophy and at the same time lost his faith in Christ." "In his declining years he was a theistic evolutionist," though "he denied God's revelation to man as well as miracles."[23]

Why, then, did Bole publish Lady Hope's letter in 1940? He does not mention changing his mind about Darwin's religious views, but merely gives the letter as below, without further comment. In any case, it is Lady Hope's fullest account, containing several new details: the circumstances of her visit(s) to Down House; a description of Darwin's room; and of course more imaginative dialogue. Also noteworthy is Lady Hope's new explanation, passed on by Bole, for her residence in the United States.

Some twenty years ago I read of the interviews that Lady Hope had with Charles Darwin during the last years of his life. Knowing that this Christian lady belonging to the English nobility was living in Los Angeles, I wrote to her asking for the story. In her reply she stated that she had left England to spend the last years of her life in California to avoid the persecution of the Darwins and their evolutionary friends. I again wrote her, promising that I should not make public her story during her lifetime, and a few days later received the following letter:

Dear Sir:

I happened to be staying with some friends of mine in a quiet village in Kent; and was told that very near their house was the residence of Dr. Darwin. Indeed, I was shown the large gate that opened on to his carriage drive; and I heard that he was scarcely able now to leave his house, or even his room. I forget in what years I was there; but it must have been some time before his death.

At this time I was holding cottage meetings in the village, and also some drawing room meetings in the large houses. These meetings were all on Gospel and Temperance lines, and consisted in every case of at least the reading of some portion of Scripture, with conversation about it.

It was at luncheon one day, that the lady with whom I was staying, said to me:

"Dr. Darwin has heard that you are here; and he would like very much to see you. He asks if you could come over this afternoon."

So it was arranged that I should call at three P.M. I should like to give you my impressions, when I first saw him.

As the door was opened on the landing upstairs, I saw him lying on a sofa beside a very fine bay window, which overlooked a most extensive view of cornfields, gardens, and scattered cottages. It was a large room with a high ceiling, and there on the sofa I saw him reaching out his hand to me. His magnificent open forehead, crowned with white hair, the earnest, almost intense look in his eyes, and his pleasing expression impressed me greatly. He had a large book open, in front of him, and one hand was on the page. It was a Bible. Raising his hand, he said most emphatically:

"This is the Epistle of Hebrews; the Royal Epistle, I call it. Isn't it so? And oh, this Book, this Book, I never tire of it."

And he began to comment on some of the great Gospel truths, which I only regret extremely, I cannot give verbatim. He spoke of Christ in this way:

"He is the King, the Saviour, the Intercessor, dying, living," and discoursed rather freely, and with great animation on the different parts of the subject.

"But what about Genesis, the very first book in the Old Testament? Your name is always associated in one's mind with certain doubts about that history—the Creation, I mean, your views?"

Here, his whole aspect changed. A look partly of anger, and partly of great distress, was on his face, as he closed his hands, throwing them forward, while he said with a sort of groan or sigh:

"I was young then. I was ignorant. I was enquiring, searching, trying to find knowledge. I wanted the truth, and there . . . and then." He hesitated, as if he was quite overcome, and burst out with a louder voice, apparently in great displeasure, "They went and made a religion of it."

He sank back quite exhausted, after this outburst, and closed his eyes. Then we talked again quietly. It was either on this occasion or another about the same time, that he suddenly turned and said to me, with a bright smile:

"Have you been in my garden? No? Then you have not seen my summer house. It is quite a large one. I should think it would hold about thirty people!

"Now, I want to know if you mould [sic] have a meeting there and talk to my people. You see there are servants and laborers, and some tenants, for there are farms on the estate; and then there are all my neighbors.

"Would you be willing to do this for me? Of course, you would sing some hymns, not the sad, old drony ones, but those others." (The Sankey hymns). "Oh, yes," he was smiling so brightly. "I cannot go myself; but this window would be open, and I could hear them all."

There was such an animated, earnest expression on his face as he said this.

"What shall I speak on," I asked.

"Oh, on the Lord Jesus Christ," he answered most earnestly.

Of course, I was willing, indeed.
But it never took place. I feel sure there was a lack of sympathy on these lines in the house.
But I can only repeat to you the imperishable memories of that glowing face, and those impassioned sentences.

Lady Hope.

Source: BOLE, BATTLEFIELD OF FAITH
(1940), PP. 166–68

The Nicholls Recollection, 1958

Born in 1860, A. H. Nicholls lived in Downe for many years before and after Darwin's death. He became the local postman, and in his eighties he had clear memories of the horse-drawn buses that used to run through the village. In 1881 he was converted through Fegan's mission. Emma Darwin marveled in letters to her son George that it wasn't only "wicked old Reeves" who "'makes prayer' . . . so does Nicholls." He went on to become "one of the oldest surviving stalwarts of the Gospel Hall congregation," which grew out of Fegan's schoolroom services. These experiences brought Nicholls in contact with "the lady who nursed Darwin," according to a friend who sent his own second-hand recollection to the press. The references in it suggest that she was none other than Lady Hope.[24]

Sixty years ago I was a schoolboy at Downe and the Darwin influence was still evident, chiefly through individuals who had been connected with Down House. Among those who had personal touch with the lady who nursed Darwin was the late Mr. A. H. Nicholls, a local tradesman and a man known for his integrity and fine Christian principles. He died last year at the age of 97.

During one of my visits to him he told me that this lady, who had been in attendance on Darwin prior to his death, had informed him that he requested her to read the New Testament to him and asked her to arrange for the Sunday school children to sing "There is a green hill far away." This was done and Darwin, who was greatly moved, said, "How I wish I had not expressed my theory of evolution as I have done."

Knowing Mr. Nicholls as I did, I have no hesitation in believing that Darwin, like many of our wise men, found the simple Gospel of Jesus Christ far more satisfying than evolution.—Leonard Fawkes, 38 Fashoda-road, Bromley.

Source: FAWKES, BROMLEY AND KENTISH TIMES,
NOV. 7, 1958, P. 12

APPENDIX B

~~~~~~~~~~~~~

THE LEGEND SPREADS, 1882–1993

~~~~~~~~~~~~~

T HIS TABLE LISTS IN CHRONOLOGICAL ORDER ALL KNOWN
texts containing full or fragmentary accounts of the
deathbed legend, and the authorities on which each
text depends. Arrangement is by date of publication except
for manuscript items in the years 1882, 1887, 1915,
1922–23, and 1925. Question marks indicate missing or
uncertain information. Publications in unknown years are
inserted at approximate dates. Full references appear in the
bibliography except for the manuscript items, which are
transcribed and documented in Appendixes A, C, and D.

	Texts	*Authorities*
1882	D. Birchall, in Verey, *Diary of a Victorian Squire*, p.137 (App. A)	sermon by "Mr Huntingdon," Tenby Parish Church, Dyfed, South Wales, May 7
1885	Cooper, *Thoughts* p. 139, (App. A)	letter of R. Eadie, Sept. 19, 1882, referring to a letter from Darwin received by his father
1887	correspondence between C. Dedûchson of the Toronto *Mail* and T. H. Huxley, Jan. 26 and Feb. 12 (App. A)	sermon by Rev. J. Mutch of Chalmers Presbyterian Church, Toronto; letter of F. Darwin, Feb. 8 (App. C)
1907	Anderson, *In Defence,* p. 95n (App. A)	Lady Hope
1915	letter of A. T. Robertson, Aug. 4 (App. A)	Lady Hope
	Watchman-Examiner, Aug. 19 (chap. 5)	Lady Hope

	Lady Hope, *Baptist World*, Sept. 9	*Watchman-Examiner*, 1915
	letter of J. L. Howe, Dec. 8	letter of F. Darwin, ? (App. C)
1916	letter of F. Darwin, ?, Jan. ?	Darwin family
	Anon., *Bombay Guardian*, Mar. 25	*Watchman-Examiner*, 1915
	Panin, *Bible Numerics*, May–June	*Watchman-Examiner*, 1915
1917	Gregory, *Honour*, June	Anon., *Bombay Guardian*, 1916
?	?, *The Gleaner*, ?	?
1920	Pollock, *British Evangelist*, Dec.	*The Gleaner*, ?
1921	Townsend, *Collapse of Evolution*	*Watchman-Examiner*, 1915
1922	Litchfield, *Christian*, Feb. 23 (App. C)	Darwin family
	Booth-Tucker, *Christian*, Mar. 9 (App. A)	Lady Hope
1922 /23	correspondence between A. P. Smith, W. J. Bryan et al., June 7 and 12, 1922; Jan. 31, 1923 (App. A)	Lady Hope
1924	Burrell, *Bible Champion*, May	?
	Anderson, *Doubter's Doubts*, 3d ed., p. 81	Anderson, 1907
	Hardie, *Evolution*, pp. 159–61	Townsend, 1921; Burrell, 1924
1925	E., *Life of Faith*, Jan. 14	?
	Viator, *Life of Faith*, Jan. 28	undated letters of F. and L. Darwin (App. C)
	Joy, *Life of Faith*, Feb. 4	Gauss, 1925
	Le Lievre, *Life of Faith*, Feb. 11	letters of F. Darwin, Nov. 27, 1917 and May 28, 1918 (App. C)
	Pollock, *Churchman's Magazine*, Mar.	Pollock, 1920
	letter of J. W. C. Fegan, May 1 (App. D)	Lady Hope; Darwin family
	Anon., *The Tablet*, May 2	Pollock, 1925
	letter of J. W. C.Fegan, May 22 (App. D)	Lady Hope; Darwin family
	Gauss, *What Some Scientists Have Said about Evolution*	?
	Pratt, *What Is Truth?*	? Gregory, 1917; letter of M. Gregory; Le Lievre, 1925; letter of A. S. Dyer, Feb. 17, 1925; letter of A. A. Gibson, vicar of Downe, Mar. 31, 1925 (App. D)

1927	Panin, *Bible Numerics,* Sept.	Panin, 1916
	Anon., *Christian Fund-amentalist,* Dec.	?
1928	Dunkin, *Local Preachers' Magazine,* Jan.	?
	Williams, *Local Preachers' Magazine,* Feb.	undated letter of B. Darwin (App. C)
	Chadwick, *Joyful News,* Mar. 8	Dunkin, 1928
	Panin, *Bible Numerics,* May–June	Panin, 1916; Dunkin, 1928; Williams, 1928; Chadwick, 1928
	Panin, *Bible Numerics,* Sept.–Oct. (App. A)	Anderson, 1907; Le Lievre, 1925; anecdote from "an Anglican Rector" about F. Max Müller and "Miss G. C."
1930	Derome, *Daily Argus-Leader,* Oct. 5, 12, 19	Argus Leader Information Bureau, Washington, D.C.; letters from editors of *Sunday School Times* and *Watchman-Examiner,* the staff of Northfield School, A. T. Robertson; letters from "members of the Darwin family," July 8 and 13, 1930 (App. C)
1933	Foote, *Infidel Deathbeds*	Pollock, 1925; F. Darwin, 1916
1934	L. Darwin, *The Times,* Aug. 15 (App. C)	Darwin family
	Protonius, *Literary Guide,* Oct.	L. Darwin, 1934
1935	Anon., *Bible Numerics,* Nov.	Panin, 1916
1937	Anon., *Literary Guide,* June	L. Darwin, 1934
1940	Bole, *Battlefield of Faith,* pp. 166–68 (App. A)	Lady Hope
1946	O.Smith, *Challenge of Life,* pp. 105–6	? Anon., *Christian Fundamentalist,* 1927
1955	Anon., *Message from God,* Oct.	Anon., *Bombay Guardian,* 1916
1956	Amos, *Reformation Review,* Oct.	Anon., *Message from God,* 1955
1957	Amos, *Monthly Record,* Feb.	Amos, 1956
1958	Johnston, *The Scotsman,* Apr. 15	? Anon., *Message from God,* 1955; Amos, 1956; Amos, 1957
	Barlow, *The Scotsman,* May 8 (App. C)	Litchfield, 1922; letter of H. Litchfield, Mar. 23, 1922
	Johnston, *The Scotsman,* May 8	? Anon., *Message from God,* 1955; Amos, 1956; Amos, 1957
	Hawton, *The Humanist,* July	Litchfield, 1922; Anon., *Message*

		from God, 1955; Amos, 1957; Johnston, 1958
	Fawkes, *Bromley and Kentish Times,* Nov. 7 (App. A)	anecdote of A. Nicholls, resident of Downe in 1880s
1959	Baxter, *Awake, My Heart,* p. 196	*Watchman-Examiner,* 1915
	Tilney, *Darwin and Christianity*	? Anon., *Bombay Guardian,* 1916; anonymous correspondents
?	?, *Christian Witness,* ?	?
1960	Sloan, *The Humanist,* Mar.	Anon., *Bombay Guardian,* 1916; Pollock, 1920; Litchfield, 1922; Booth-Tucker, 1922; Johnston, 1958; Barlow, 1958; Fawkes, 1958
1962	Naismith, *1200 Notes, Quotes*	*Christian Witness,* ?
1965	Sloan, *The Humanist,* Apr.	Sloan, 1960
1966	Enoch, *Evolution or Creation*	Anon., *Bombay Guardian,* 1916
?	?, *Prayer Crusade,* ?	O. Smith, 1946
1967	Amos, *Good Tidings,* May–June	Amos, 1956
?	Anon., *Evolution Theory Examined*	?
1968	Myers, *Voices*	*Prayer Crusade,* ?
1969	Royer, *Advocate of Truth,* Feb. 3 (see App. F)	? Darwin, *My Apology for My Unformed Ideas,* ?; O.Smith, 1946
	?, *The Sword and Staff,* Oct.	? Royer, 1969
	Anon., *Bible-Science Newsletter,* Dec.	*The Sword and Staff,* 1969
	Davidheiser, *Evolution and Christian Faith,* pp. 66–69	?
1970	Royer, *Truth and Liberty,* May (see App. F)	Royer, 1969
	Tilney, *Charles Darwin*	Anon., *Bible-Science Newsletter,* 1969
1971	Davidheiser, *Science and the Bible*	?
1974	Atkins, *Down,* pp. 51–52	Booth-Tucker, 1922; Sloan, 1960; Sloan, 1965
1975	Anon., *National Educator,* July	undated tract: O.Smith, *Darwin, "The Believer"*
	Rusch, *Creation Research,* Sept.	undated tracts: Anon., *Darwin's Last Hours;* Pollock, *Charles Darwin's Deathbed*
?	? *Standard of Truth,* ?	? O. Smith, 1946
1977	Anon., *The Flame,* Jan.–Feb.	*Standard of Truth,* ?
	Freeman, *Works of Charles Darwin,* pp. 19, 119	Royer, 1970; Atkins, 1974

1978	Freeman, *Charles Darwin*	Atkins, 1974
	Pearce, *New International Dictionary*	?
1979	Phippin, *Radio Times*, Jan. 12–19	?
	Turner, *"Creation,"* July	letter of L. G. Pine
1982	Smith, *United Holiness Sentinel*, Mar.	O. Smith, 1946
	Stone, *New Scientist*, Apr. 8	?
	Bowden, *Rise of the Evolution Fraud*	Enoch, 1966; Rusch, 1975; Turner, 1979
?	MacAlister, *Scientific Proof of Origins*	?
?	Pastor Mel, *Faith Seed*, ?	?
1983	Hedtke, *Secret of the Sixth Edition*	?
1984	Burrowes, *North American Creation Movement Newsletter*, ?	?
	Rusch, *Creation Research*, June	Anon., *Christian Fundamentalist*, 1927; Hawton, 1958; Rusch, 1975; Turner, 1979; Bowden, 1982
	Clark, *Survival of Charles Darwin*, pp. 98–99	Litchfield, 1922; Atkins, 1974
	Taylor, *In the Minds of Men*, pp. 136–37, 450	Anon., *National Educator*, 1975; Turner, 1979
1986	McIver, *Skeptical Inquirer*, spring	Hawton, 1958; Tilney, 1959; Enoch, 1966; Tilney, 1970; Turner, 1979; Bowden, 1982; MacAlister, 1983; Burrowes, 1984; Rusch, 1984; Taylor, 1984; Jimmy Swaggart telecast, Sept. 30, 1984; Wally George's "Hot Seat" telecast, Jan. 12, 1985
	Anon., *Bible-Science Newsletter*, Dec.	?
	Brown, *Evolution of Darwin's Religious Views*, p. 27n	Clark, 1984
1988	Rusch and Klotz, *Did Charles Darwin Become a Christian?*	Rusch, 1975; Rusch, 1984
1989	Anon., *Berean Ambassador*, July	O. Smith, 1946
	Croft, *Life and Death*, pp. 105–20	Fawkes, 1958; Sloan,1960; Sloan, 1965; Atkins, 1974; Freeman, 1977; Stone, 1982; Clark, 1984
1990	Herbert, *Darwin's Religious Views*	Anon., *United Holiness Sentinel*, 1982; Bowden, 1982; Clark, 1984;

		Taylor, 1984; Anon., *Berean Ambassador*, 1989
1992	Newman, *Creation Research*, Sept.	*Watchman-Examiner*, 1915; Rusch, 1975; Rusch and Klotz, 1988; Herbert, 1990
1993	Currey, *Evening Telegram*, Aug. 7	? O. Smith, 1946

APPENDIX C

DARWINIAN DENIALS, 1887–1958

THE DARWINS CONSISTENTLY DENIED THE DEATHBED LEG-
end, and rightly so. Any claim about a deathbed
scene, a recantation, or a religious conversion was
indeed a "work of imagination" (Francis Darwin), an "absurd fiction" (Bernard Darwin), or a "myth" (Nora Darwin
Barlow). But to go further, as the family did, and dismiss
Lady Hope's original story as a "pure invention or hallucination" (Leonard Darwin), with "no foundation whatever"
(Henrietta Darwin Litchfield), was hazardous, given that
none of the deniers but Bernard was living full-time at home
when the alleged interview(s) with Darwin took place. And
Bernard was then a child. Nor in 1915 or 1916, when Lady
Hope's story first came to the family's attention, was *any*
adult alive who had been regularly present in Down House
during 1881–82 except perhaps the Darwins' younger
daughter Bessy, an intelligent but pathetic misfit.[1]

Nevertheless the following letters have the ring of authority, with sad overtones of injured family pride; and it is
regrettable that they ever had to be written. Full references
to the original sources are given in the bibliography.

Francis Darwin to T. H. Huxley, 1887

When Thomas Huxley, Darwin's self-appointed attorney-
general, learned of Rev. John Mutch's sermon (App. A) he did
not dismiss the report out-of-hand but, with wonted rectitude,

turned immediately to his friend's third son Francis, editor of the official *Life and Letters*, for an authoritative denial.

Feb 8 1887

Dear Mr Huxley

I am glad you think it worth while to answer the Toronto man. By all means answer as you propose. You have my authority that the statement is false and without any kind of foundation.

Yours very truly
[signed] Francis Darwin

Source: HUXLEY PAPERS, 8:67

Francis Darwin to J. L. Howe, 1915

James Lewis Howe, a chemistry professor at Washington and Lee University, Lexington, Virginia, wrote immediately to Francis Darwin after he read Lady Hope's account. The reply is quoted in Howe's letter to Prof. A. T. Robertson of Southern Baptist Theological Seminary, whom he addressed as Lady Hope's "sponsor" (App. A). In a further letter to Robertson, Howe confided, "I doubt the reliability of Lady Hope's story, and yet I am also inclined to doubt its being manufactured 'out of whole cloth.' There is nothing in the letter of Sir Francis which would preclude the possibility of Lady Hope having called upon Charles Darwin in his later years, or that she may have seen him with a Bible, or that he may have enjoyed reading the Bible."[2] Robertson's replies have not been found.

Neither I nor any member of my family have any knowledge of her (Lady Hope) or of her supposed visits to Down which is quite obviously a work of imagination. He could not have become openly and enthusiastically Christian without the knowledge of his family, and no such change occurred.

Source: A. T. ROBERTSON CORRESPONDENCE

Francis Darwin to [A. Le Lievre?], 1917–18

A. Le Lievre, secretary of the Protestant Press Bureau, may not have been the recipient of Francis's next two letters but the originals were "in my possession," he said. The second letter mentions a "public" accusation, possibly in 1916, which has not been located.[3] Note that the practice of referring inquirers to the official family version of Darwin's religious life is now established.

Sir,—

I have to-day received your letter dated November 23. Lady Hope's account of her interview with my father is a fabrication, as I have already publicly pointed out. I have no reason whatever to believe that he ever altered his agnostic point of view, as given in my "Life of Charles Darwin" (in Vol. I., p. 55).

> *Yours faithfully,*
> *Francis Darwin.*
> *10, Madingley Road, Cambridge.*
> *November 27, 1917.*

Sir,—

Lady Hope's account of my father's views on religion is quite untrue. I have publicly accused her of falsehood, but I have not seen any reply. My father's agnostic point of view is given in my "Life and Letters of Charles Darwin," Vol. I., pp. 304–317. You are at liberty to publish the above statement. Indeed, I shall be glad if you will do so.

> *Yours faithfully,*
> *Francis Darwin.*
> *Brookthorpe, Gloucester.*
> *May 28, 1918*

Source: LE LIEVRE, *LIFE OF FAITH*, FEB. 11, 1925, P. 152

Henrietta Darwin Litchfield
to [*The Christian?*], 1922

In early 1922 the editors of *The Christian*, an inter-denominational evangelical weekly, were "requested to insert a contradiction, from the pen of the eldest daughter of Charles Darwin," of a "highly-coloured story . . . going the round of the American papers, with reference to the death-bed of Charles Darwin." "Occasional allusion has been made to the subject in periodicals published at home," they added squeamishly, "though it would seem, from reliable information that the story is altogether a fabrication." *The Christian* was dead-set against evolution; the editors acknowledged that "many who followed the investigations of Charles Darwin, and observed his devotion to scientific research, would have been glad to learn that some higher and deeper devotion claimed his soul." But "if there is no evidence that such was the case, it is well that the facts should be known." One "fact" to emerge from this letter is that, after her brother Francis's assertion in 1915 (above) that no member of the family had "any knowledge of Lady Hope" or her "supposed visits to Down," Henrietta was now sufficiently briefed to insist that *whether or not* Lady Hope had met her father, she had "no influence over him."

I was present at his deathbed. Lady Hope was not present during his last illness, or any illness. I believe he never even saw her, but in any case she had no influence over him in any department of thought or belief. He never recanted any of his scientific views, either then or earlier. We think the story of his conversion was fabricated in [the] U.S.A. In most of the versions hymn-singing comes in, and a summer-house where the servants and villagers sang hymns to him. There is no such summer-house, and no servants or villagers ever sang hymns to him. The whole story has no foundation whatever. His last words may be found in my book: "Emma Darwin: A Century of Family Letters." (John Murray).

Source: LITCHFIELD, THE CHRISTIAN, FEB. 23, 1922, p. 12

Francis and Leonard Darwin
to [Viator?], [1925 or earlier]

Like Le Lievre (above), "Viator" of Muswell Hill, north London, did not state that letters from Francis and Leonard (the second youngest Darwin son) were addressed to him, but only that they "lie before me." He begins by quoting Francis.

"You will see" (in *"Charles Darwin,"* edited by the writer) *"that he describes himself as an agnostic, not an atheist. You will see that he cannot accept the arguments for Christianity; but he always speaks respectfully of that faith. . . . You will see that what he says on religion was written not very long before his death."* Leonard writes: *"Some of my family looked into certain statements which were attributed—I do not know whether rightly or wrongly—to a Lady Hope, and they came to the conclusion that they were a mass of fabrication."*

Source: VIATOR, *LIFE OF FAITH*, JAN. 28, 1925, P. 93

Bernard Darwin to C. F. Williams,
[1928 or earlier]

After the death of the elder Darwin offspring, Francis and Henrietta, "Mr. C. F. Williams, B.Sc.," a Fellow of the Geological Society, writing from Hawarden, Chester, asked Francis's only son to counter Lady Hope's story, "so obviously a fake." Bernard Darwin was born at Down House in 1876 and lived there until he was about seven, so he could report only the family tradition.[4]

Dear Sir—

Thank you for your letter. I do not know how the absurd fiction about my grandfather and Lady Hope ever arose. I have been asked about it before, and so was my

father in his life-time, and other members of the family. It
is, of course, a lie, as I should think any reasonable per-
son would know, and your suspicions are entirely well-
founded.

> *Yours faithfully,*
> *Bernard Darwin*
> *Downe, Kent*

Source: WILLIAMS, *LOCAL PREACHERS'*
MAGAZINE, FEB. 1928, P. 44

[Leonard] Darwin to J. A. Derome, 1930

In 1930 J. A. Derome, associate editor of the Sioux Falls,
South Dakota *Daily Argus-Leader*, wrote a lively twelve-part
column "Was Darwin an Atheist?" for his college-town read-
ers. The latter installments show the investigative journalist
at work. No one to date had uncovered more specific details
about Lady Hope and her story. Derome corresponded with
the editors of the *Watchman-Examiner* and the *Sunday School
Times*, a staff member at Moody's Northfield School, and
Prof. A. T. Robertson. All confirmed Lady Hope's "unrelia-
bility as a writer." The Northfield informant stated that "Lady
Hope was never invited to speak under the auspices of that
institution. She was there, and spoke at the meetings of her
own accord, without any invitation from the school authorities or those in charge of the services, to take part in them."
When Prof. Robertson vouched for Lady Hope he was "sincerely repeating her story" before he "knew the facts."[5]
Robertson himself, rewriting history, assured Derome, "I did
not and do not sponsor Lady Hope's story. I knew nothing at
all about her, though she was in the audience when I spoke."
One of the Darwin sons had written to him and "flatly denied" her account. Not satisfied, Derome ran the lead to
ground. He appealed directly to "members of the Darwin

family living in England" for the final word. Lady Hope's story was "a complete fiction," wrote one; and in a second letter, after commenting on the story, Leonard added:

You are, however, entitled to say that a son of Charles Darwin has declared that Lady Hope's account of what took place at Down is entirely devoid of truth, being a pure invention or hallucination; and you may show this letter privately to any one.

Source: DEROME, *DAILY ARGUS-LEADER*,
OCT. 19, 1930, P. 6

Leonard Darwin to *The Times*, 1934

Leonard, the Darwins' last surviving child, was indefatigable: a military man and former Liberal-Unionist MP who campaigned tirelessly for "eugenic reform"—laws to promote better human breeding—though he himself was childless.[6] In religion he was a secularist, which showed in his weary denials of Lady Hope's story. The latest known, in the London *Times*, was the most widely circulated, being twiced picked up by the secularist press (App. B).

Dear Sir,—

As I grow older my faith in the veracity of mankind gets steadily less and less, and now in my eighty-fifth year it is small indeed. Nothing has added more to this decay than the anecdotes which I have heard from time to time about my father, Charles Darwin.

For example, a lady who knew the family well published a statement soon after his death that his little dog Polly had died of grief at that event, when as a fact she had been mercifully put out of her bodily pain at my mother's request. Some years later on, an eminent man of science said to me that he knew my "father well; good fellow; smoked a pipe"—which he never did. A doctor in good practise abroad told me that he had attended a course of lectures "given by Darwin" at Edinburgh: another pure invention. And a certain lady sent to the Press a long and purely fictitious account of the scene at his death-bed.

And now in your issue of August 14, Dr. Elizabeth Sloan Chesser adds another to this list when she repeats the fable that Mrs. Huxley "found Professor Huxley holding the baby and Darwin pricking it with a pin and recording its reactions to pain on a piece of paper": an anecdote on the inaccuracy of which anyone who knew either of these two men well would willingly stake their all.

> *Yours faithfully,*
> *Leonard Darwin.*
> *Cripps Corner, Forest Row, Sussex,*
> *Aug. 14.*

> Source: L. DARWIN, THE TIMES,
> AUG. 15, 1934, P. 11

Nora Darwin Barlow
to *The Scotsman,* 1958

Born in 1885, Nora Barlow was the last child of the Darwins' youngest son Horace and the first scholarly editor of her grandfather's manuscripts.[7] In 1958, having just published the unexpurgated *Autobiography of Charles Darwin,* with the "damnable" bits restored, she spied the old evangelical slur in the correspondence columns of *The Scotsman.* Her reply paraphrases a private letter from her aunt Henrietta that marks a further development in the family's recollections of Lady Hope after the publication of Booth-Tucker's testimony (App. A). Francis was indeed resident in Down House, from 1876 to 1883, but his correspondence with his father suggests that he was absent for much of the time in 1881 when Lady Hope could have visited (App. E).

Boswells, Wendover, Aylesbury
May 5 1958

Sir,—

The correspondence that has arisen in "The Scotsman"
over Charles Darwin's alleged visit from Lady Hope is per-
petuating a myth that was authoritatively denied in 1922
by those in the best position to judge of its truth or falsity.

Charles Darwin's daughter, Mrs Litchfield, wrote to "The
Christian," February 23, 1922:—"I was present at his
deathbed. Lady Hope was not present during his last ill-
ness, or any illness. I believe he never even saw her, but in
any case she had no influence over him in any department
of thought or belief. He never recanted any of his scientific
views, either then or earlier. We think the story of his con-
version was fabricated in the U.S.A. In most of the versions
hymn-singing comes in, and a summer house where the ser-
vants and villagers sang hymns to him. There is no such
summer house, and no servants or villagers ever sang hymns
to him. The whole story has no foundation whatever."

Mrs Litchfield also wrote in a letter to a correspondent
on the same subject (March 23, 1922) that she believed that
Lady Hope never had any interview with her father. She says
that her brother, Sir Francis Darwin, who was living in
Down House at that time, was certain that Lady Hope never
came to the house.

Charles Darwin was no controversialist, but I think he
would approve of this refutation of a false myth, as the ed-
itor of "The Christian" said in February 1922, "in the in-
terest of truth."—I am &c.

Nora Barlow.

Source: N. BARLOW, THE SCOTSMAN,
MAY 8, 1958, p. 6

APPENDIX D

MR. FEGAN PROTESTS, 1925

I N THE MONTHS BEFORE HIS DEATH J. W. C. FEGAN (1852–1925) was twice asked to pronounce on Lady Hope's account of her visit to Down House at the time of his village mission over forty years earlier. J. A. Kensit, head of the militant Protestant Truth Society, forwarded to him an article by Maurice Gregory akin to his 1917 piece in *Honour*, which drew on the original *Watchman-Examiner* story as published in the *Bombay Guardian*. S. J. Pratt of Forest Hill, south London, sent his own tract, *What Is Truth? Was Charles Darwin a Christian?*, which reprinted a letter to him from the vicar of Downe, Alfred A. Gibson, who in 1911 had succeeded the last incumbent of Darwin's lifetime, Rev. George Ffinden. Fegan's replies, though repetitive, each contain enough new matter to justify printing them in full. Gibson's letter to Pratt is reproduced below, before Fegan's reply to the same.

The replies to Kensit and Pratt were dictated to Fegan's private secretary, A. W. Tiffin, and duly typed. Tiffin, then twenty-two years old, kept carbon copies, and in 1977 he quoted the less personal portions in a typescript letter to Rev. A. Sowerbutts, editor of *The Flame*, in which a version of Lady Hope's story had just appeared. A year later a copy of this letter, a typescript copy of the missing passages, and a copy of Pratt's tract were supplied by Tiffin to my colleague Colin Russell of the Open University. Tiffin granted that "at this distance of time, and in the interests of truth, I

153

have no objection to your discretionary use of all the information I have given you." Thanks to Prof. Russell, Fegan's replies have been reconstructed and are published here for the first time.[1]

Fegan's reliability as a witness, no less than Lady Hope's, is open to question. His arguments may be judged on their merits, and in the light of the evidence given in chapters 4 and 5. Note that Fegan claims only that "the interview as described by Lady Hope, and the service she said she was asked to hold in the summer-house, never took place." He does not deny that she worked in Downe or even that she may have visited and spoken with Darwin.

J. W. C. Fegan to J. A. Kensit, 1925

To Mr. J. A. Kensit of the
Protestant Truth Society,
1st May 1925.

[Dear Mr. Kensit,]

I have just read Mr. Gregory's article,[2] but I cannot find in it a single fact in support of Lady Hope's story. At the top of page 106 I read: "But mark this fact . . . for thirty years he was the right-hand helper of the Vicar of Downe." Now, I lived with my father and mother at Downe in 1880 and spent all the time I could spare from my work at Deptford with my mother in her widowhood, from January 1881 till 1883,[3] and you may take it from me that Mr. Darwin was not on speaking terms with the then Vicar of the Parish— Mr. Ffinden—a very boorish man who did not even exchange "good morning" with a passing parishioner, and by his rude manners drove away from the Church not only the Darwin family, but the Lubbock family as well.

All through the summer of 1881 I held services in a tent in Downe.[4] When it was getting too late for tent services, and as the only available room in which to continue them was a Reading Room established by Mr. Darwin (an old schoolroom which he rented from Sir John Lubbock but very little used by the villagers), I asked Mr. Darwin if he would lend it to me for Sunday evenings. He did so with pleasure. A few weeks afterwards I asked him if he would let me have the use of it for a week's Mission. He replied to this effect: "Dear Mr. Fegan, You ought not to have to write to me for permission to use the Reading Room. You have far more right to it than we have, for your services have done more for the village in a few months than all our efforts for many years. We have never been able to reclaim a drunkard, but through your services I do not know that there is a drunkard left in the village. Now, may I have the pleasure of handing the Reading Room over to you? Perhaps, if we should want it some night for a special purpose, you will be good enough to let us use it. Yours sincerely, Charles Darwin." In that Reading Room, now called "The Gospel Room," services have been held continuously for the last 44 years. The services I held were attended sometimes by members of the Darwin family, and regularly by members of their household. Indeed, whenever I held a Mission in Downe, the Darwin family were considerate enough to alter their dinner-hour so that their household might attend—but this was characteristic of their relationships with all who served them. At the services I held, Parslow—the old historic family butler, whose name you will find mentioned by Huxley, Wallace, etc., was converted to God, and brought into Church membership; also the housekeeper, Mrs. Sales, was brought into the light—and others.

Mr. Gregory's suggestion of an interview between Darwin and "a passing friend" would be rejected by anyone who knew how closely Mr. Darwin was safeguarded by Mrs. Darwin, his family, and the servants, from all callers. I have been appealed to several times about this story by those who knew my connection with the village of Downe, and have always said what I am sure everybody else would say who was living in Downe during Mr. Darwin's lifetime—that the interview as described by Lady Hope, and the service she said she was asked to hold in the summer-house, never took place. As a matter of fact, there never was a summer-house, in which a service could be held, in the grounds! And when Sir Francis Darwin says that Lady Hope's story is a fabrication, that denial is quite enough for anybody who knows the high standards of truth which the Darwins inherited from their father.

There were three great naturalists living in the neighbourhood of Downe when I was there—Mr. Darwin, Sir John Lubbock (afterwards Lord Avebury), and Mr. Dresser, the great ornithologist. There was a good deal of petty persecution on the part of some "purse-proud" London manufacturers, etc. and farmers in the neighbourhood; but these three gentlemen stood by me and folks who came to our services very gallantly. Mr. Darwin gave his support, not because he believed the truths I sought to proclaim, any more than he believed the truths the South American Society was seeking to spread in Patagonia. He helped them and me because he recognised the results of the work they and I had done.⁵

I think the point where you, Mr. Gregory, and others have been led astray in this matter is that you are not acquainted with the facts of the later part of Lady Hope's life. If you were, I think you would not find the fabrication of this story so unbelievable. I knew Lady Hope when she was Miss Cotton, and also her saintly father and mother, Sir Arthur and Lady Cotton. I never knew Sir Henry [sic] Hope, her first Husband; but her second husband, Mr. T. A. Denny, was an old friend of mine, and he gave me his confidence in the last year or two of his life—as to what he had suffered from Lady Hope. Indeed, it was the revelations that Lady Hope was running a River-club unknown to him that brought about his death! I presume that you know that, some years after Mr. Denny's death, Lady Hope was adjudicated bankrupt.

When she was leaving here for America, she asked me to give her a commendatory letter to use in America, and I had the painful duty of telling her I could not do so.

If you make enquiry, I think you will find that the final paragraph of Mr. Gregory's article is misleading, for this reason—that Lady Hope did not get a hearing at any recognised gathering at Northfield, but for the first time told her startling story to some friends assembled in a private house in the neighbourhood, while the Northfield Convention was being held. Naturally, the story spread, and she was asked to repeat it in other places she visited. Why had she not told it in England? I do not see that the cause of truth can be served by perniciously circulating a story the truth of which has been combated over and over again; and as regards poor Lady Hope, I think the kindest course is to let the story sink in oblivion.

I am quite sure that anybody who knew Mr. Charles Darwin would agree with me that he is one of the last men we have ever known, if he thought a lot of people had been misled by any theories or suggestions of his, to pass away without in the fullest and most public manner, acknowledging any mistakes on his part in his suggestions, or in the way he had phrased them. There is no question that Mr. Darwin died as he had lived—an agnostic—but he was a most honourable, chivalrous and benevolent gentleman. If you get "The Letters of Emma Darwin" (his wife, who was a Christian), edited by her daughter, Mrs. Leifchild, [sic] you will find two very beautiful letters which she wrote her husband at two periods in their married life, in which she acknowledges the honesty with which he was making his diligent research into Nature, but begging him to give revealed truth its due share of his consideration. I consider them literary models of tender, wifely pleading. By the way, you will find a passing allusion to the services I was holding, in which she refers to the account brought home by her housekeeper, Mrs. Sales, of a prayer-meeting she had been

*at where the old village blacksmith—a notorious drunk-
ard—had prayed beautifully![6]*

*I have marked this "Confidential," because I do not want
to be drawn into any further controversy, nor do I want my
name published in connection with the Darwin family. I
strongly resent the way in which it has been sought to exploit the name of Darwin in circulating this story, in face of
the denial of his family and others, who are competent to
judge from first-hand experience whether there is any probability in the story or not.*

With kindest Christian regards, I remain, dear Mr. Kensit,

Yours sincerely,
J. W. C. Fegan

Source: A. W. TIFFIN, NORTH ADELAIDE,
AUSTRALIA, VIA COLIN RUSSELL

A. A. Gibson to S. J. Pratt, 1925

The Vicarage, Downe, Kent,
March 31, 1925.

Dear Mr. Pratt,

*Thank you for the copies of the tracts received this morn-
ing. I have not received an answer from Miss Ffinden, the
only surviving member of the family of my predecessor, who
was Vicar of Downe when Charles Darwin died, but I have
seen and talked over the points with the very few old in-
habitants whose memories go back to the critical date.*

*The evidence obtainable tends to prove beyond question
that whatever may have been Darwin's innermost attitude
towards revealed truth in his later days and at the time of his
departure, no such interview, as imputed to Lady Hope's testimony ever took place. The Story was published many years*

*ago in "The Christian," and apparently came first from
America. Mrs. Lichfield, [sic] Darwin's Daughter, who was
with him through his final illness, wrote to deny the statements, and her letter was published in the "Christian," with
a brief note appended by the Editor to the effect that it was
a pity it was not true.[7] There never was a Summer-house of
the size named in the garden of Downe House; and certainly
nothing was ever heard of a gathering being held or proposed
to be held there by Lady Hope. I regret that I have to give
you what will be disappointing information. But after all,
though one would have rejoiced to be able to affirm that Darwin held the essential truth after all, [omission?] and it may
still have been so. Yet the loss of the touching Story is not
material, for there is our Lord's statement as to the effective
power of even the most startling evidence. Luke XVI.31.*

> *Believe me, yours very truly*
> *Alfred A. Gibson.*

Source: PRATT, WHAT IS TRUTH? WAS
CHARLES DARWIN A CHRISTIAN

J. W. C. Fegan to S. J. Pratt, 1925

To Mr. S. J. Pratt,
3 Beadnell Road,
Forest Hill, London, S.E. 23,
22nd May 1925.

Dear Mr. Pratt,

*Thank you very much for the copies of Mr. Gibson's let-
ter, and also for your kind letter of yesterday.*

*I think the difficulty you and some others feel is through
your not knowing the character of Lady Hope's later life,
and through your not knowing what I have understood to
be the genesis of the story in question—which "The Tablet"*

of a few weeks ago truly characterised as "pathetic but mendacious," and uses as an illustration the recklessness with which the Protestant Controversialists seek to support any cause they are advocating.

In the first place, after her marriage with Mr. T. A. Denny, Lady Hope should have been content to be known as Mrs. T. A. Denny, and it was only vanity on her part to cling to the title of "Lady Hope," as I think all her friends were driven to the conclusion that it was only vanity which led her in the first place, as a girl of, I suppose, about 24 or 25, to marry old Sir Henry [sic] Hope who, I imagine, was between 70 and 80.[8]

I do not think I over-state the case when I say that Lady Hope broke Mr. T. A. Denny's heart. The climax of her extravagance came when he discovered that, unknown to him, she was running a River Club. He went down to see it, and was seized with illness, which necessitated his lying on a water bed until he passed away.

About two years or so after his death she was adjudicated bankrupt. I daresay a couple of years or so after that, she wrote to me asking me to give her a commendatory letter to take with her to America, and it was my painful duty to tell her that I did not feel I could do so.

I have been given to understand that she sought to get a hearing at the Northfield Convention, but did not succeed. She was, however, during the Convention, asked to a house where there was a large party of guests, to whom she told this startling story, which became a current topic at the Convention.

The editor of some periodical was much impressed, and asked her to put the story into writing, which she did, and anybody familiar with Lady Hope's style can recognise it in the current version of the story.

As it is known to many that I was living with my mother in Downe from 1880–83 and had, so to speak, the village in the "hollow of my hand" through Tent services there, and in the adjoining villages; and that Mr. Darwin transferred to me, for the continuance of these services, when the season got too late for Tent meetings, his Reading Room which had been a failure (in which Gospel services have been continued up to the present day); I have been appealed to over and over again as to the probability of this story, and have had no hesitation in pronouncing it to be a fabrication on the part of poor Lady Hope.

You are quite right that Mr. Darwin never poured scorn on the Christian faith. He was one of the last men in the world to stoop to pouring scorn upon anybody's conscientious belief. He was an honourable, courteous, benevolent gentleman; but you may be sure that Sir Francis Darwin is right in saying that his father died as he had lived—an agnostic.

Strangely enough, about a week ago, I was reading the life of the late Lord Guthrie. In it, he describes a visit to Andrew Carnegie at Skibo Castle. Among his fellow-guests was Lord Morley. After dinner the subject of talk was "Truthfulness." John Morley said that he had intimately known two—and only two—men of real eminence who were absolutely truthful—John Stewart [sic] Mill and Charles Darwin. Carnegie suggested Martineau. "No," said John Morley. "Martineau would keep on arguing in favour of a theory of his after he must have known it was proved to be false; but Mill or Darwin would at once acknowledge they had been mistaken, and own their opponents were right."

If you can get hold of "The Letters of Emma Darwin," edited by her daughter, Mrs. Leifchild, [sic] you will find two beautiful, wifely letters from Mrs. Darwin (who was a sincere Christian), in which she recognises the honesty of her husband in his research into Nature, but pleads with him to give revealed truth its right place in his thoughts.

Parslow, the old historic butler of the Darwin family, was brought into the light, and into Church fellowship, through my services; so was Mrs. Sales, the housekeeper in the Darwin family, and other servants; so that I was in close touch with the Darwin household. It may further interest you to know that whenever I held a Mission in Downe, even after I had ceased to reside there, the Darwin family used to do what I have never known another family in their position do—alter their dinner-hour so that their household might be free to come to my services.

But all this is no more evidence that either Mr. Darwin or his family agreed with the truths which I was seeking to preach than his subscription to the South American Missionary Society, after what he had seen of their work amongst the Patagonians long years ago, is any evidence of his agreement with the truths they were teaching. Mr. Darwin recognised—as Professor F. W. Newnham, [sic] another agnostic, went out of his way, some years ago, in a conversation with me, to recognise—the influence of Christian life and teaching upon the hearts and habits of men and women.

As to co-operation with the Vicar of Downe, Mr. Darwin would have co-operated with anybody in any kindly effort for the good of his neighbours; but, as a matter of fact, I do not believe he was ever on speaking terms with Mr. Ffinden— an exceptionally boorish man, who would not exchange even "good morning" with any parishioner; and whose bad manners drove away both the Darwin family and the Lubbock family from attending their Parish Church.

I have marked this letter "Confidential" because you will understand I am weary of discussing the veracity of this preposterous story, and do not want my name to be used any further in connection with it.

Charles Darwin is the last man I can conceive of who, after finding that any had been misled by any theoretical suggestion of his, would pass away without the most public acknowledgment of his regret that his suggestions had influenced minds beyond what he had intended. He was, in all his dealings, public and private, a noble, chivalrous character.

I can ill afford the time to write at such length, but I do so out of respect for the honesty with which I am sure you

*have persisted in seeking to clear up what I can well under-
stand has seemed to you a "mystery."*

*Please allow me to say, in conclusion, that I knew Sir
Arthur and Lady Cotton well, and treasure the memory of
their saintly characters; and that I have never had an unpleasant word with Lady Hope. Up to the end, we were on
friendly terms, although, of course, I had considerable uneasiness about her sayings and doings, both in her husband's
lifetime and afterwards; and I very earnestly wish that for
her sake this story might now be allowed to sink into oblivion. It cannot in any way be used to serve the cause of "the
scripture of truth."*

With kindest Christian regards,

> *Yours in Eternal Bonds,*
> *J. W. C. Fegan.*

*Postscript. Have you ever considered why Lady Hope be-
tween 1882–1916 never told this striking story in England?—why she never cleared her name from Sir Francis
Darwin's charge of falsehood? Lady Hope passed away I
think it must be nearly two years ago in California.*

> Source: A. W. TIFFIN, NORTH ADELAIDE,
> AUSTRALIA, VIA COLIN RUSSELL

APPENDIX E

WHEN DID LADY HOPE VISIT DOWN HOUSE?

I F LADY HOPE'S STORY WAS BASED ON AN ACTUAL INTERVIEW with Darwin, when could they have met? The evidence suggests a striking coincidence.

Given that Fegan's mission centered on Downe village in 1881, and assuming that Lady Hope carried on the work during his sick-leave, sometime between July and October, we can place her in the vicinity of Down House from the arrival of hop-pickers in September, when her coffee tent was needed (chap. 4). That year the Kent harvest was slow to start because of a "long and unbroken period of unseasonably cold, wet weather" in the latter part of August. Most of September was rather dry, cold, and dull, with showery and fair days alternating, but by the 17th the hop harvest was in full swing. It usually lasted three to four weeks—we may assume that a full month was needed because of the bad weather.[1] By early October, then, the coffee-tent phase of the mission ended.

So if Lady Hope was present in and around Darwin's parish throughout September 1881 and possibly into October, on which day or days might she have seen him? The only clue is in the first version of her story: "it was on one of those glorious autumn afternoons . . . he was gazing out on a far-stretching scene of woods and cornfields, which glowed in the light of one of those marvelous sunsets which are the beauty of Kent and Surrey." On which days, then,

165

after "three P.M." according to Lady Hope's last account (App. A), was such a scene likely to be visible from Darwin's west-facing bedroom window?

Three sets of records in the National Meterological Archive help narrow the dates.

First, the rainfall registers from stations at Beckenham and Bromley Common, north of Downe, at Westerham and Sevenoaks to the south, and especially at Leaves Green, two miles west by northwest of Down House (near the present-day Biggin Hill aerodrome), clearly show two periods of almost dry weather, from September 12 to 18, and from September 27 to October 6.

Second, the exhaustive "Addiscombe Meterological Observations" made near Croydon, Surrey, about nine miles northwest of Downe, show that at 3 P.M. daily there was sunshine, sometimes with haze or scattered clouds, on September 14 and 16–18, and from September 28 to October 4. The sun shone on average over seven hours a day in both periods.

Third, the weekly weather reports issued by the Meterological Office in London confirm that in both periods high pressure prevailed over southeast England, with clearing fog and "very fine" or "bright" skies almost everywhere. At adjacent intervals conditions were deteriorating or poor.

In which period, then, was Lady Hope likely to have revelled in the splendid weather as she visited Darwin? She says that they met on an "autumn" afternoon, so strictly speaking it was on or after September 21. Two further considerations also point to this period.

First, Francis Darwin, who then lived in Down House, was present both for his uncle Erasmus's funeral on September 1 and for Aveling and Büchner's visit on the 28th— "a day that summer seemed to have left behind," as Aveling recalled. Meanwhile Francis' son Bernard celebrated his fifth birthday and Darwin himself made out a new will, reapportioning his sons' inheritance.[2] Both activities would naturally have required Francis' presence, although in any case he had left home by Saturday, October 1.[3] Since he later claimed to be "certain that Lady Hope never came to the house" (App. C), he may have been absent on the day or days she allegedly called. The visit's *terminus a quo* would thus be Wednesday, September 28.

Second, Fegan—who had not returned to Downe by mid-September at least—was back the very next Sunday preaching to "crowded congregations."[4] Since he later pronounced Lady Hope's story to be a "fabrication" (App. D), it is entirely possible that he too was absent at the time she met Darwin. The visit's *terminus ad quem* would thus be Sunday, October 2.

Further than this it is unsafe to conjecture. The present evidence, however, points to a striking coincidence (if it is a coincidence): Lady Hope could have called on Darwin in the immediate aftermath of his postprandial discussion with Aveling and Büchner. He did not instigate the atheists' visit to Down House but he did start that discussion. By contrast, he did invite Lady Hope to call (according to her private accounts) and was found reading the Bible. Since Emma was reportedly present on both occasions, and a clergyman sat beside her at the atheists' luncheon, it may be that, to mollify her afterwards, Charles sent for Lady Hope.

On Sunday October 2 Emma wrote to her devout daughter Henrietta about the comings and goings at Down House since her previous letter on September 21. She named at least eight visitors and mentioned "the beautiful weather (now for a week)" but said not a word about Aveling and Büchner at lunch on Wednesday. Nor was the clerical guest mentioned, nor indeed Lady Hope.[5] Emma, mindful of Henrietta's own sensitivities, perhaps drew a veil discreetly over both fraught visits.

Appendix F

Darwin's "Other Book"— The End of the Trail?

I N DECEMBER 1980 I ESCAPED FROM A WORLD MOURNING John Lennon and drove solemnly into the snow-clad mountains of West Virginia. My purpose was to find a rare, unrecorded book; my destination, the small town of Salem, headquarters of the Church of God (Seventh-day) and home to Chris Royer, editor of the denomination's magazine, *The Advocate of Truth*.[1] In 1969 Royer published an article there claiming that his father once loaned him a book entitled *My Apology for My Unformed Ideas*, in which "Darwin denied everything he had ever written concerning his 'Origin of Species.'" The book was composed "right after he came to his senses while in a sanitarium where he had been placed for loosing [sic] his faculties." Darwin is reported to say, "I became like King Nebuchadnezzar, of the Book of Daniel, a wild and insane creature. God punished me by making me senseless and when I came to I realized I must write and correct the wrongs I had committed."[2]

Darwin's bibliographer R. B. Freeman did not "believe that the work exists or ever did exist." Nor did I. But Freeman had sent me a reprint of Royer's article from the magazine *Truth and Liberty* (published in New South Wales "for God, Queen, and Country"), with an appended note by the author that made me think again. Maybe Darwin's "other book" (as Royer called it) was a real book that somehow "grew" from the story started by Lady Hope. Hadn't Royer said in his article that he remembered the book only after reading the words she attributed to Darwin, "I was a young man with unformed ideas"?

Royer's note stated that *My Apology for My Unformed Ideas* "is out of print. It can be found only in second-hand book stores. I believe the enemy of truth has tried his best to destroy this information. My father brought a copy with him from a Seminary in Germany and has kept it as a rare treasure."[3] This galvanized me. I ransacked the U.S. *National Union Catalog* and the great libraries at Cambridge, Oxford, and the British Museum. Not a single reference to Darwin's "other book" turned up. I would have to find the Royers' copy.

Chris met me at the *Advocate of Truth* office. He showed me around the press, then took me home and introduced his wife and his mother Maria. After a brief inquisition—"do you keep the commandments, observe the Sabbath, etc.?"— they warmed to their overseas guest and even welcomed my note-taking.[4] All were helpful, sharing memories and family documents, though important items seemed to be missing or mislaid. My own questions were answered frankly, with total aplomb. I sensed that the Royers believed themselves to be "advocates of truth."

The first thing I learned was that Chris's father, Charles L. Royer, died in 1952, aged seventy. Born in Germany, he had gone to college at Magdeburg, married Maria in 1919, and emigrated with her and their infant son, Chris, a few years later. They settled in New Haven, Connecticut, where Charles became treasurer of the New England Conference of Seventh-day Adventists; he left them in 1930 to join the Church of God (Seventh-day). Afterwards he obtained a Ph.D. in theology from Columbia University—an academic hood was produced in evidence—and served as a Church of God minister, moving "back to Salem" in 1949 with the denominational headquarters. On his father's death Chris inherited his large theological library, which was much in evidence as we spoke: fat Teutonic tomes scattered among countless tracts and late Victorian titles, including anything and everything "seventh-day." Not the typical private collection in the Alleghenies.

Chris, born in 1920, had been an army surgical technician during the War—"just like M.A.S.H.," he chuckled. He then studied biblical subjects briefly at Leeds University before returning to Salem in 1946 to finish his education at the local Seventh-day Baptist college. He had married in town and worked there ever since, chiefly for the denomination. As a hobby he wrote the history of seventh-day movements from his huge, hand-me-down library.

So did he still have Darwin's "other book"? Chris shook his head and shrugged: it had turned up missing about eight years before, when the print shop was renovated. In fact, he seemed unsure whether he had written the 1969 *Advocate of Truth* article from memory. But of course he remembered the book very well, having handled it often. So did his mother, whom I interviewed separately. Maria came from an educated Alsatian family; at eighty she was alert and articulate, though she still spoke with a heavy accent. She told me that Chris first read the book as a teenager. It had survived a house fire in 1937 and then he had inherited it with the library. Neither of them had been able to find it for about ten years.

I asked them each to describe *My Apology for My Unformed Ideas*. Chris, who learned the printing trade from his father, gave graphic details. It was a small cloth-bound octavo, about five inches by eight, "plain," gray-looking, without embossing or other decoration except perhaps gilt-edges. It had about 150 pages, with cuts of Darwin, his home, and his friends made from crude linoleum or wood engravings. It was printed in English and published in the 1900s, whether in Britain or Germany he could not recall.

Maria confirmed that the book was gray. It used to sit beside a green one the same size by Huxley. They were always
shelved together, Huxley and Darwin. When I asked Chris
to show me the Huxley book he seemed relieved. He went
straight to a shelf and came back clutching a small green octavo entitled *Evolution and Regeneration*. It was, I pointed
out, a treatise on occult science by Henry Proctor, and published by L. N. Fowler, the London phrenologist. Sheepishly,
Chris offered it to me as a sort of consolation prize.

Well, then, had either of them seen or heard of other
copies of *My Apology for My Unformed Ideas*? Oh yes,
Chris brightened. He thought his father had said that L. R.
Conradi owned one. The two of them were "just like brothers" at Magdeburg. Conradi became president of the Eu-
ropean Conference of Seventh-day Adventists, then followed Royer into the Church of God as the Nazis came to
power. Hitler "broke his heart," Chris recalled. Maria, who
had known Conradi personally, explained. As a sabbatar-
ian he was suspected of being Jewish and so prevented from
opening a new church. He retreated to his Hamburg house,
in Grindelberg-strasse, and spent his last years alone, attended by a housekeeper. But at least he had the company
of a fine library, Maria smiled. When he died in 1939 everyone wanted it.

I had heard all the Royers could tell me. The next day Chris
took me to Moore's Restaurant for breakfast. I thanked him
warmly and drove back to a world where "Lennon lives!" t-
shirts were already on sale. Personally, I had reached a dead-
end. My interest in Darwin's "other book" was finished. Such
a book no more existed for me than John Lennon did a fortnight after his murder, though legends about each —the book
and the Beatle—might live on.

For I have little doubt that *some* book formed the basis
of the Royers' recollections, just as I have come to believe
that an actual meeting between Darwin and Lady Hope
lay at the root of the deathbed legend. The book in ques-

tion had belonged to Chris's father, and perhaps his friend Conradi had also owned a copy. If anyone now wishes to track the book down, it seems that the Conradi library will have to be found. Did he in fact possess a fine library? Did it survive the War? If so, where is it today? Does it contain a volume answering to the Royers' description? I leave these questions to those with the will and the means to pursue them.

NOTES

Foreword

1. "The Present Status of the Doctrine of Evolution," *The Presbyterian Messenger,* 3, no. 10 (Dec. 5, 1895), pp. 7–8.

Ghosts, Coffins, and Ladies

1. "Outlook"; L. Huxley, "Huxley's Attitude"; Dreyer, *Gardener,* p. 276; Clark, *Life,* p. 791; F. B. Smith, "Atheist Mission," pp. 230–31; Foote, *Infidel Death-beds; Death's Test;* Mann, *Science and the Soul.* Cf. Lewis, *Modern Rationalism,* chap. 10.

2. Lady Hope, "Darwin and Christianity."

3. Russell, *Their Religion,* pp. 273, 296–97; Coxe, *Haunted Britain,* pp. 78–79.

4. Colp, "Charles Darwin's Coffin"; Smithers, "Charles Darwin's Wandering Coffin."

5. Sloan, "Demythologizing Darwin," pp. 106, 109; O. Smith, "Why I Am against Evolution" (source of the "Northfield, England" version); McIver, "Ancient Tales" (for Jimmy Swaggert's "Lade Hope"), Currey, "Good Word" (for "Lady Pope"); Rusch and Klotz, *Did Charles Darwin Become a Christian?* pp. 13–14 and Taylor, *In the Minds of Men,* p. 137 (for Emma as Lady Hope). The "Lady

Ogle" story was started by Rev. J. J. Dyck, a former missionary to India with the Mennonite Brethren Mission, who spent his later years in Canada working with the Central City Mission, Vancouver. So wrote Mr. J. A. Guenther in letters to Ralph Colp Jr. (Apr. 14, 1976) and myself (Aug. 27, 1984). Guenther claimed to have known Dyck "quite intimately" and reported his saying that he received the story from Lady Ogle herself. Though there were "no written testimonies concerning the incident," Dyck was "not the kind of man who would spread a fairy tale." Guenther also forwarded to me (May 19, 1984) a letter written to him by Mr. A. Naismith of Falkirk, Stirlingshire (May 29, 1976), who vouched for the trustworthiness of both "Rev. Dick" and Lady Ogle. Naismith claimed to have known the lady—"since deceased"—"very well" and was "satisfied that she would not make a personal statement—in which she was involved personally— that was not true. Of course, we can also take into consideration that she might not in old age remember very accurately what happened when she was a youngster." If any of this thirdhand hearsay can be trusted, it is the last statement, which rules out identifying Lady Hope with Lady Ogle. Lady Hope

175

was nearly forty years old when she allegedly met Darwin. A woman named Ogle perhaps appropriated her story and repeated it to Rev. Dyck.

6. Birth certificate of Elizabeth Reid Cotton, Registrar-General, Hobart, Tasmania, 1843, no. 618; Lady Hope, *General Sir Arthur Cotton*, pp. 23, 24, 40–41, 151, 172, 498; obituaries of General Sir Arthur Cotton, *Times* (London), July 26, 1899, p. 10 and July 31, 1899, p. 6; "Admiral Sir James Hope"; "Mr. T. Anthony Denny"; death certificate of Elizabeth Reid Hope, Registry of Births, Deaths and Marriages, Sydney, 1922, no. 1554; will of Elizabeth Reid Hope, Principal Register of Probate, London, 1923, no. 297.

7. Keith, *Concerning Man's Origin*, p. 6n.

8. Sloan, "Myth" and "Demythologizing Darwin"; Atkins, *Down*, p. 109; Rusch and Klotz, *Did Charles Darwin Become a Christian?* p. 20; Anon., "Questions and Answers." Tipped off by Turner's article, "Darwin and Lady Hope," a series of creationist writers have allowed that Elizabeth Reid Cotton, alias Lady Hope, *might* have been the source of the deathbed legend: Bowden, "Return to Faith"; Rusch, "Darwin's Last Hours Revisited"; Taylor, *In the Minds of Men*, pp. 136–37, 450; Herbert, "Deathbed Repentance"; and Newman, "Darwin Conversion Story," p. 71. Only Croft, *Life and Death*, pp. 112–14, firmly identifies her as the source of the deathbed legend, but for paltry reasons.

9. An indefatigable Darwin legend buster, Rev. Burton K. Janes of Howley, Newfoundland, has written to me (Oct. 13, 1993 and Jan. 4, 1994) about one in his church who stood to "testify," enthusing that "Darwin had converted before he died." He had "heard about it that morning on TV."

1 A Man in Conflict

1. Full documentation for this chapter, with further detail, is available in my works listed in the bibliography, especially Desmond and Moore, *Darwin*.

2. McCalman, "Popular Religion" gives the best account of Taylor's career.

3. Thomson and Rachootin, "Turning Points."

4. Desmond, *Politics of Evolution*.

5. Desmond, "Robert E. Grant."

6. Rudwick, "Charles Darwin in London."

7. Sulloway, "Darwin's Conversion"; Barrett et al., *Charles Darwin's Notebooks*, p. 291 (C166).

8. Manier, *Young Darwin*; Erskine, "Darwin in Context."

9. Burkhardt and Smith, *Correspondence*, 1:512, 2:443; Colp, *To Be an Invalid*, pp. 14–20 and "Charles Darwin's Dream."

10. Barrett et al., *Charles Darwin's Notebooks*, pp. 224–25 (B214, 216), 276 (C123), 309 (C220), 536–37 (M73–74), 608–9 (OUN26–29).

11. Barrett et al., *Charles Darwin's Notebooks*, p. 343 (D36–37); C. Darwin and Wallace, *Evolution by Natural Selection*, p. 87.

12. Secord, "Discovery of a Vocation"; Barrett et al., *Charles Darwin's Notebooks*, p. 263 (C76).

13. Burkhardt and Smith, *Correspondence*, 2:352; Howarth and Howarth, *History*; Atkins, *Down*. The village changed the spelling of its name to Downe in the mid-nineteenth century to avoid confusion with County Down in Ireland. Down House retained the old spelling.

14. Barlow, *Autobiography*, p. 95; Burkhardt and Smith, *Correspondence*, 2:123, 131, 172; John 15:6 (KJV).

15. Colp, *To Be an Invalid*, pp. 20–34.

16. Burkhardt and Smith, *Correspondence*, 3:2, 43, 85, 258; Colp, "'Confessing a Murder.'"

17. Colp, *To Be an Invalid*, pp. 35–53 and "Charles Darwin's 'insufferable grief.'"

18. Burkhardt and Smith, *Correspondence*, 4:140.

19. Burkhardt and Smith, *Correspondence*, 6:178; Colp, "Charles Darwin's Reprobation of Nature."

20. Stecher, "Darwin-Innes Letters"; J. Marsh, "Charles Darwin."

2 A Family Divided

1. Portions of this chapter have been adapted from Desmond and Moore, *Darwin*. For full documentation and further detail, see also my works listed in the bibliography.

2. Barrett et al., *Concordance*; C. Darwin, *Origin*, pp. 459, 490; Mayr, *One Long Argument*.

3. Peckham, *Origin*, pp. 40 (*1.1:b*), 748 (*183.3:b*); Young, *Darwin's Metaphor*, chap. 4; Kohn, "Darwin's Ambiguity"; Beer, *Darwin's Plots*.

4. Desmond and Moore, *Darwin*, pp. 481, 486; Burkhardt and Smith, *Correspondence*, 7:390.

5. Desmond and Moore, *Darwin*, pp. 487–88; Burkhardt and Smith, *Correspondence*, 7:396–97, 399; Litchfield, *Emma Darwin*, 2:172, 175; Colp, *To Be an Invalid*, p. 120.

6. Desmond and Moore, *Darwin*, p. 500; Moore, *Religion*, p. 437.

7. Recollections of F. Darwin, Darwin Archive 140.3:23; C. Darwin to F. Abbot, May 27 and Nov. 16, [1871], Harvard University Archives; Ahlstrom and Mullins, *Scientific Theist*, pp. 72–80, 88ff.

8. F. Darwin, *Life and Letters*, 1:91; Colp, *To Be an Invalid*, p. 104. Emma also helped with the local children's temperance group, the Band of Hope,

which sometimes met at Down House. See Stecher, "Darwin-Innes Letters," p. 248; E. Darwin to G. Darwin, Aug. 18, 1881, Darwin Archive 210.3; and Shiman, "Band of Hope Movement."

9. Burkhardt and Smith, *Calendar*, no. 7124; Litchfield, *Emma Darwin*, 2:196.

10. Litchfield, *Richard Buckley Litchfield*. The corrected proof sheets of Darwin's "Preliminary Notice" for Ernst Krause's *Erasmus Darwin*, showing Henrietta's cuts, are in Darwin Archive 210.10. The deleted footnote, as corrected, reads: "I have heard from a connection of the family that an old and faithful maid-servant, who was present when my grandfather died, afterwards told his step-daughter, that on hearing him faintly saying something, she bent down her head to listen, but the only word she caught was 'Jesus.' This was an inexpressible comfort to his step-daughter (from whose daughter I have received this account), and she spoke of it only a few weeks before her own death. But it is incredible that my grandfather should have wholly changed his judgment on so important a subject, and that my father should never have heard of it, though he hastened to Derby on the news of his father's death. The good old maid-servant must have fancied that she heard what she wished to hear; and the statement may be added to the many apocryphal death scenes on record. That comfort should be derived by relations from a change in the settled convictions of a life-time, just when sense and reason are failing, is a strange fact, but seems to be part of human nature."

11. N. Barlow, *Autobiography*, pp. 85–96; Desmond and Moore, *Darwin*, chap. 41.

12. E. Darwin to W. Darwin, [Sept. 13, 1876], Darwin Archive 210.6.

13. W. Darwin to F. Abbot, June 13, [1880], Harvard University Archives; recollections of F. Darwin, Darwin Archive 140.3:24, which agrees.

14. Banks, *Victorian Values*.

15. C. Darwin to C. Bradlaugh, June 6, 1877, Darwin Archive 202; Desmond and Moore, *Darwin*, pp. 627–28.

16. Desmond and Moore, *Darwin*, pp. 642–45; E. Aveling to C. Darwin, Oct. 12, 1880, Darwin Archive 159; C. Darwin to E. Aveling, Oct. 13, 1880, transcribed in Feuer, "Is the 'Darwin-Marx Correspondence' Authentic?" Darwin's reply was long assumed to have been addressed to Marx: see Colp, "Contacts of Charles Darwin" and "Myth of the Darwin-Marx Letter."

17. Tribe, *President Charles Bradlaugh*, pp. 210–11, 358; F. Darwin and Seward, *More Letters*, 1:395; E. Aveling to C. Darwin, Aug. 9, 1881, and C. Darwin to E. Aveling, Aug. 11, [1881], both Darwin Archive 202.

18. F. Darwin and Seward, *More Letters*, 1:395, 2:433.

19. E. Darwin to G. Darwin, Sept. 28, 1881, Darwin Archive 210.3.

20. Aveling, *Religious Views*, pp. 4–5; Desmond and Moore, *Darwin*, pp. 656–58.

21. F. Darwin, *Life and Letters*, 3:358.

22. Desmond and Moore, *Darwin*, pp. 664–73.

3 The Compromise

1. Foote, *Darwin on God*, pp. 22–23; Royle, *Radicals*, pp. 32–34.

2. "Sugar Plums"; Aveling, in *National Reformer*, n.s., 39 (Apr. 30, 1882), p. 339.

3. Recollections of F. Darwin, Darwin Archive 140.3:112–13; Leonard Darwin to *The Times*, 1934, App. C; B. Darwin, *World*, p. 20; recollections of H. Darwin, Darwin Museum.

4. Litchfield, *Emma Darwin*, 2:253–56; Burkhardt and Smith, *Correspondence*, 3:326; recollections of H. Darwin, Darwin Museum.

5. Burkhardt and Smith, *Correspondence*, 2:445 n. 7; Litchfield, *Emma Darwin*, 2:261; Emma's book of extracts, quoted in Montgomery, "Emma Darwin."

6. Browne, "Charles Darwin–Joseph Hooker Correspondence," pp. 357–58.

7. See *Deutsche Rundschau* and *Frankfurter Zeitung* for Sept. 19, 1882; Haeckel, *Naturanschauung*, pp. 48, 60 n. 17 (translation); and *Pall Mall Gazette*, Sept. 23, 1882, p. 2.

8. See reports and correspondence in *The Academy*, 22 (Oct. 14, 1882), p. 279; (Oct. 21, 1882), p. 296–97; (Oct. 28, 1882), p. 314; (Nov. 4, 1882), p. 330, as well as Lewins, "Mr. Darwin and Professor Haeckel." Cf. the transcription of the English original obtained by Francis Darwin and certified by Mengden and Haeckel, in Darwin Archive 139.12. The original letter reads: "For myself, I do not believe that there ever has been any Revelation. As for a future life every man must judge for himself between conflicting vague probabilities."

9. "Hitherto Unpublished Letter"; "Charles Darwin on Religion"; Haeckel, "Professor Haeckel on Darwin," p. 540; Aveling, "Visit." The Oct. 29 issue of the *National Reformer* also reprinted Darwin's letter to N. D. Doedes from a Dutch freethought paper, *De Dageraad*. In it Darwin suggested that the existence of God is "beyond the scope of man's intellect." Cf. the autograph copy, dated Apr. 2, 1873, in Darwin Archive 139.12.

10. Litchfield, *Emma Darwin*, 2:261.

11. Barlow, *Autobiography*, p. 87n; Burkhardt and Smith, *Correspondence*, 2:172.

12. Correspondence of F. and W. Darwin, Darwin Archive 210.8, and of L. Darwin, Darwin Archive 112:19–22.
13. Keynes, *Leonard Darwin*, p. 42; correspondence of F. and W. Darwin, Darwin Archive 210.8.
14. Draft by F. and W. Darwin in re E. Darwin, Darwin Archive 210.8.
15. E. Darwin to W. Darwin, Jan. 20 and "Monday" [after Jan. 20], 1885, Darwin Archive 219.1; Barlow, *Autobiography*, p. 93n; Litchfield, *Emma Darwin*, 2:270, 279–80 and 1904 ed., 2:360; F. Darwin, *Life and Letters*, 1:26, 69, 307; Moore, "Of Love and Death."
16. Arnstein, *Bradlaugh Case;* Freeman, *Works*, p. 173; Browne, "Charles Darwin-Joseph Hooker Correspondence," p. 353.
17. F. Darwin, *Life and Letters*, 1:317n.
18. Barlow, *Autobiography*, p. 95; F. Darwin, *Life and Letters*, 3:359; correspondence of F. and W. Darwin, Darwin Archive 210.8.
19. Dawson, *Indictment*, pp. 35–36; Bradlaugh and Besant, *National Secular Society's Almanack*, p. 7.

4 Evangelical Innuendoes

1. N. Barlow, *Autobiography*.
2. F. Darwin, *Life and Letters*, 3:358. Rumors of Bradlaugh's recantation on his 1891 deathbed were still circulating in the 1920s (Bradlaugh Papers 3350–52, 3356, 3360, etc.). But his daughter had ready replies, having taken minute precautions to procure signed testimony from those who attended him, that during his last illness he never uttered a word bearing directly or indirectly on religion (Foote, *Infidel Death-beds*, p. 25).
3. The TenbyTale, App. A.
4. The Eadie Note, App. A.
5. The Toronto Sermon, App. A.

6. "Mr. T. Anthony Denny"; "Late Mr. T. A. Denny"; Booth, "Late Mr. T. A. Denny"; Kinnaird, *Reminiscences*, pp. 38–39; recollections of Lavender Harington, typescript, pp. 1–4, Denny Family Papers; scrapbook, "Messrs Moody & Sankey's London Mission 1883–84," Moody Museum.
7. "Lawyer, Author, Evangelist"; Moore-Anderson, *Sir Robert Anderson* and *Sir Robert . . . and Lady Agnes*, pp. 35–64, 91, 97; Coad, *History*, pp. 222–23.
8. Lady Hope, *General Sir Arthur Cotton;* J. Brown, "Sir Proby Cautley," pp. 70–81.
9. Lady Hope, *General Sir Arthur Cotton*, pp. 24, 167–74, 496–98; Braithwaite, *Life and Letters*, pp. 330–31.
10. Lady Hope (i.e., E. R. Cotton), *Our Coffee-Room*, pp. 12, 195 and "Coffee Rooms"; Heasman, *Evangelicals*, p. 138. For background, see Dingle, *Campaign* and Shiman, *Crusade*.
11. Mackinnon, *Recollections*, pp. 30–100 passim; "Hope, Sir James"; Lady Hope, *Lines of Light*, "Trained Nursing," "What Shall We Do," and *English Homes*, p. 159; "New Coffee Tavern"; "Old Beckenham Mission." For background, see Prochaska, *Women and Philanthropy* and Malmgreen, *Religion*.
12. Moore-Anderson, *Sir Robert Anderson*, pp. 83–85 and Moore-Anderson, *Sir Robert . . . and Lady Agnes*, p. 77; Fegan, "Personal Tribute"; "'A Life for Souls'"; Fullerton, *J. W. C. Fegan*; Spivey, "James Fegan."
13. Whitehead, *Hops*, pp. 18–19 and *Hop Cultivation*, p. 35; Stratton, *Hops and Hop-pickers*, pp. 160–63, 170–85; J. B. Marsh, *Hops and Hopping*, pp. 80–81; Harvey, "Fruit Growing"; "Kent in the Hop-picking Season"; "Hop-picking."

14. *Bromley Directory*; Fullerton, *J. W. C. Fegan*, pp. 29–30; Stecher, "Darwin-Innes Letters," p. 247.

15. "Tent Services at Bromley"; "Down, Orpington, Kent"; E. Darwin to H. Litchfield, [May 1880], Darwin Archive 219.2.

16. Darwin to J. Fegan, [late 1880], in Fullerton, *J. W. C. Fegan*, p. 30. The previous winter Fegan gave Tuesday evening temperance "lecture[s]" in the reading room, "interspersed with tea drinkings." The Darwins' maids brought back rave reports, delighting Emma: "I think a little enthusiasm in this dead village may do real good" (E. Darwin to H. Litchfield, [Feb. 1880?] and Feb. 25, 1880, Darwin Archive 219.2).

17. "Notes and Comments"; Mr. Fegan Protests, App. D; Litchfield, *Emma Darwin*, 2:244 (E. Darwin to H. Litchfield, [Jan. 1881?], Darwin Archive 219.2); E. Darwin to G. Darwin, Jan. 31 and Feb. 8, 1881, Darwin Archive 210.3; Fullerton, *J. W. C. Fegan*, p. 31.

18. "Mr. Fegan and His Work"; E. Darwin to H. Litchfield, Sept. 13, 1881, Darwin Archive 219.2; Clinch, *English Hops*, p. 39; *Extraordinary Tithe Charge*, passim; *Report from the Select Committee*, pp. 1133–34, 2785.

19. "Admiral Sir James Hope"; Lady Hope, *Our Golden Key*, pp. 104–13. For recollections of late Victorian charities among the hoppers, see Thompson, "Medical and Social Work."

20. Cf. The Toronto Sermon, App. A and Mr. Fegan Protests, App. D.

21. T. A. Denny account book, Denny Family Papers; Moore-Anderson, *Sir Robert . . . and Lady Agnes*, pp. 87, 126; Sir Robert's Evidence, App. A.

22. E. Denny to L. Legge, July 9/15, 1906, Denny Family Papers; will of Admiral Sir James Hope, Scottish Record

Office, C380, p. 170; Lady Hope, "Lady Hope's Appeal"; Mr. Fegan Protests, App. D; The Hope Bandeau Ltd, Public Record Office BT31/19027/105294; "A Widow's Affairs." Official details are in High Court of Justice in Bankruptcy: Index 10, Jan. 1, 1911–Dec. 31, 1913; and Register of Receiving orders, 1911–12.

23. "Praises English Queens"; "Lady Hope Praises Glories of Newport"; Lady Hope, "Halls of Happiness"; death certificate of Elizabeth Reid Denny, known as Hope, Registry of Births, Deaths and Marriages, Sydney. For background, see Hammerton, *Emigrant Gentlewomen*.

5 Lady Hope's Story

1. Mabie, *Years Beyond*; Carter, *So Much to Learn*; Laws, "Northfield Conference" and "Summer Days."

2. A. T. Robertson, "Glory of Jesus"; "Defend Orthodoxy."

3. Mott, *History*, p. 138; Doctor Bob's Report, App. A; Lady Hope, "Darwin and Christianity."

4. But Sloan, "Myth," p. 72, suggests that of all the books in the Bible "the Epistle to the Hebrews . . . is an open attempt to present Christianity in an evolutionary light, as the logical development of Judaism. Darwin might have been discovered reading Hebrews with very great interest, not as a convert, but as an evolutionist," just as he had read Francis Newman's *History of the Hebrew Monarchy* in 1849 (Burkhardt and Smith, *Correspondence*, 4:479). The Darwin family Bible preserved in the Darwin Museum is unmarked except for an unattributable small, backwards pencil tick opposite the early verses of Hebrews 6.

5. Keith, "Neglected Darwin," pp. 5–6; F. Darwin, *Life and Letters*,

1:121–22; recollections of F. Darwin, Darwin Archive 140.3:6, 8; Litchfield, *Emma Darwin*, 2:76, 86, 95; A. J. Skinner, the former Downe schoolmaster, in Abbott, *Twelve Great Modernists*, p. 248; Atkins, *Down*, p. 34; Sloan, "Demythologizing," p. 109. Strangers occasionally turned up in the summerhouse; Raverat, *Period Piece*, p. 157, mentions a "drunken tramp." After 1859, according to George Darwin's recollections (Darwin Archive 112:22), "the principal wooden pigeon house was erected as a sort of elevated summer house above the tool house at the near end of the kitchen garden." The structure would probably have been visible from Darwin's upstairs window, from where Lady Hope described the view. But it was "overgrown with a splendid mass of ivy" and unsafe; "during a gale in the Spring of 1882 it was badly blown over." Darwin would never have offered it to her. As a child years later Raverat called it "the Poison House" (*Period Piece*, p. 159).

6. In the first volume of *Life and Letters* Francis Darwin published his own reminiscences of his father: he wore "dark clothes, of a loose and easy fit" (p. 112); "about three in the afternoon, he rested in his bedroom, lying on the sofa and smoking a cigarette, and listening to a novel or other book not scientific" (p. 121); "when walking he had a fidgeting movement with his fingers" (p. 110); and "when he was excited with pleasant talk his whole manner was wonderfully bright and animated, and his face shared to the full in the general animation . . . he was given to gesture, and often used his hands in explaining anything" (pp. 111, 112).

7. Darwin not only resisted Aveling's atheistic extrapolations (chap. 2); he quailed at Haeckel's political pantheism and generally bemoaned the Germans'

"foolish idea . . . on the connection between Socialism and Evolution through Natural Selection." See Desmond and Moore, *Darwin*, pp. 538–43 and F. Darwin, *Life and Letters*, 3:237.

8. Guest Book, 1910–16 ("property of Isaiah Moody Esq."), Moody Museum; Lady Hope, "Halls of Happiness"; Derome, "Weekly Meditation," pt. X; will of Elizabeth Reid Hope, Principal Register of Probate, London, 1923, no. 297.

9. The Los Angeles Affidavit, App. A.

10. Lady Hope's Last Words, App. A.

11. Booth-Tucker's Testimony, App. A; obituaries in *Daily Telegraph* (Sydney), Mar. 10, 1922, p. 6 and *Times* (London), Mar. 14, 1922, p. 15; "Lady Hope."

12. Litchfield, *Emma Darwin*, 2:251. Attempts to date Lady Hope's interview with Darwin point to a striking coincidence: see App. E.

13. Shaftesbury, "Preface," in Lady Hope (i.e., E. R. Cotton), *More about Our Coffee-Room*, p. viii; Keith, "Neglected Darwin," pp. 5–6; Atkins, *Down*, pp. 23, 35. Three women were regarded as Darwin's personal friends: Miss Arabella Buckley, a naturalist and secretary to Charles Lyell, and Mrs. Jane Lushington and Miss Laura Forster, friends of Henrietta (recollections of F. Darwin, Darwin Archive 140.3:64). Darwin felt real affection for Miss Forster. She never forgot an encounter with him in the month before he died, when she was convalescing at Down House: "I remember one day was the 1st time that I was able to walk at all, I left the verandah & walked once or twice up and down the path to the dining room window. Your father happened to come to his bedroom window above the dining room and saw me, & he opened the window at once, & leaned out of it to say, 'that is right dear

Laura, it does me good to see you walking about again.' I was pleased to see that tho' a bad day he had vigour eno' to yield to his impulse of opening the window so readily" (L. Forster to F. Darwin, Nov. 15, 1885, Darwin Archive 112:38–39).

6 Legends Alive

1. Laws, "Convention Side Lights," p. 834.
2. The Los Angeles Affidavit, and Lady Hope's Last Words, both App. A.
3. Darwinian Denials, App. C.
4. Henrietta Darwin Litchfield to [*The Christian?*], App. C. The family did release additional information in a pair of two-volume works. In 1903 Francis Darwin and A. C. Seward's *More Letters of Charles Darwin*, a collection of scientific correspondence, contained "practically all the matter that it now seems desirable to publish," according to the editors (1:viii). Henrietta Litchfield's "century of family letters," *Emma Darwin*, was printed for private circulation in 1904 and published in 1915, omitting materials of "purely private interest" (1:ix).
5. Panin, "Darwin Dies a Christian," p. 7.
6. F. Darwin to [A. Le Lievre?], 1917–18, App. C; Foote, "Charles Robert Darwin"; The Los Angeles Affidavit, App. A.
7. Keynes, *Leonard Darwin;* Moore, "On the Education"; L. Darwin, *What Is Eugenics?* pp. 7, 68, 75.
8. C. Darwin, *Descent*, pp. 617–18; Spencer, *Piltdown;* Keith, *Autobiography*, p. 400, "Some Anthropological Notes," p. 182, and *Concerning Man's Origin*, pp. 48, 49, 54.
9. Keith, *Autobiography*, p. 435, "Neglected Darwin," pp. 3, 7–9, and *Concerning Man's Origin*, p. 39.

10. Royle, *Radicals*, pp. 165–67; Lightman, "Ideology, Evolution," pp. 286–88; Huxley, *Charles Darwin*, p. 113 (cf. Huxley, "Home Life," p. 6); Moore, "On the Education," pp. 64–65.
11. Whyte, *Story*, p. 96; Keith, *Autobiography*, pp. 489, 509, 523n, 633 and *Religion*, pp. 70–71; Atkins, *Down*, p. 111.
12. Keith, *Concerning Man's Origin*, p. 7 and *Autobiography*, pp. 506–7, 523; Atkins, *Down*, pp. 112–25.
13. Atkins, *Down*, p. 115; Keith, *Concerning Man's Origin*, p. vii, *Autobiography*, pp. 507, 509, and *Darwinism*, pp. v, 21, 55–56; L. Darwin, *What Is Eugenics?* p. 88.
14. Atkins, *Down*, pp. 115–17; Keith, "Darwin Remembered," p. 21 and *Autobiography*, p. 522; L. Darwin, "Memories," p. 118. The Darwins "hated" the stuffed Polly, but after a few years the moths had done their worst and it mercifully had to be destroyed (B. Darwin, *World*, p. 20).
15. Keith, *Autobiography*, pp. 530–31 and "Darwin Remembered," pp. 22–25.
16. Bennett, *Natural Selection*, pp. 81, 98, 121; Whyte, *Story*, pp. 74–78; Freeman, *Works;* L. Darwin, "Memories," p. 121; Kent, *London for Heretics*, p. 128.
17. "Rationalist Press Association Annual Dinner," p. 125; Keynes, *Leonard Darwin*, p. 42; Keith, "Some Anthropological Notes," p. 182 and *Darwin Revalued*, p. 268; Leonard Darwin to *The Times*, 1934, App. C; Protonius, "Another Darwin Myth"; Anon., "Myths about Darwin."
18. Johnston, "Like Darwin, I doubt"; Barlow, *Autobiography*, pp. 11–12; Nora Darwin Barlow to *The Scotsman*, 1958, App. C.

19. Hawton, "Personally Speaking"; Pike, "Darwin of Downe"; Sloan, "Myth," pp. 71–72 and "Demythologizing Darwin," pp. 106, 109–10.

20. Rusch and Klotz, *Did Charles Darwin Become a Christian?* p. 21; Rusch, "Darwin's Last Hours Revisited"; Taylor, *In the Minds of Men,* pp. 136–37; Herbert, "Deathbed Repentance"; Atkins, *Down,* pp. 51–52; Croft, *Life and Death,* pp. 112, 114, 120. Newman, "Darwin Conversion Story," correctly identifies Lady Hope and reproduces her original *Watchman-Examiner* story for the first time in eighty years.

21. Gay, *Bourgeois Experience,* pp. 403–60.

Appendix A
Sources of the Legend

1. Verey, *Diary,* pp. ix–xiii; B. and H. Wedgwood, *Wedgwood Circle,* p. 306; Litchfield, *Emma Darwin,* 2:193–94, 220; Desmond and Moore, *Darwin,* p. 655.

2. Royle, *Victorian Infidels,* p. 309; "Eadie, John," *Encyclopaedia Britannica,* 11th ed.

3. Only Mandelbaum, "Darwin's Religious Views," p. 364 n. 10, has noted the Dedûchson letter.

4. *Register of the University; Calendar of Knox College,* p. 36; J. Robertson, *Landmarks,* pp. 278–80; J. R. Mutch, *Genealogy,* p. 72; "Rev. John Mutch." See also *Annual Report* in Metropolitan Toronto Central Library. According to the Toronto *Globe,* Mutch was to have been in his pulpit every Sunday from Dec. 5, 1886 through Jan. 23, 1887, for services at 11 A.M. and 7 P.M. No record of the sermon has been found. The "Session Minute Books" of the congregation date from September 1891; the earlier ones were probably lost in the fire that destroyed the main

church building in January 1945. J. Mutch, "Hosea's Conception of God's Feelings towards Israel," is the only publication found.

5. J. R. Mutch, *Genealogy,* p. 74; Scroggie, *Story;* Mackinnon, *Recollections,* pp. 121, 128, 167, 176, 231, 247. In March 1884 a James Scroggie became one of the first elders to be added to Chalmers Presbyterian Church under Mutch's ministry. See *"Fifty Years of Progress,"* p. 8 in the Church Archives.

6. Fullerton, *J. W. C. Fegan,* chap. 10. On the exploitation of the immigrant orphans, see Parr, *Labouring Children,* and Bean and Melville, *Lost Children.*

7. *College Y.M.C.A. Souvenir,* p. 22, in YMCA Historical Library. On the spirit and significance of the 1886 conference, see Findlay, *Dwight L. Moody,* pp. 346–52 and Tatlow, *Story,* pp. 17ff.

8. On Feb. 10 and 11 Wallace was to lecture on "The Darwinian Theory" and "Origin and Uses of Color in Nature," according to the Toronto *Standard,* Feb. 8, 1887, p. 4. Wallace, *My Life,* 2.125–26 places the lectures in March.

9. Moore-Anderson, *Sir Robert Anderson,* pp. 83–85, 98, 116 and *Sir Robert . . . and Lady Agnes,* pp. 87, 126, "Lawyer, Author, Evangelist"; Fegan, "Personal Tribute"; Coad, *History,* pp. 222–23.

10. McKnight, "A. T. Robertson's Contribution"; A. T. Robertson, "Glory of Jesus"; "Bible Study Courses"; Gill, *A. T. Robertson,* p. 129.

11. "Defend Orthodoxy"; A. T. Robertson, "Prohibition Movement," "Darwinism and the South," and "Evolution and Modern Science"; Gill, *A. T. Robertson,* p. 181.

12. Unusually, the Aug. 6, 1915 *Springfield Daily Republican* devoted only four column-inches to the General Conference. Robertson is not mentioned.

13. A. T. Robertson, "Scientists." For Robertson's interlocutors, see letters from J. D. Eggleston, Sept. 20, 1915; R. J. McBryde, Sept. 29, 1915; J. L. Howe, Nov. 24 and Dec. 8, 1915; W. S. Plumer Bryan, July 17, 1916; S. T. Brosius, Aug. 18, 1919; and J. A. Derome, Oct. 1, 1930, A. T. Robertson Correspondence (no replies have been found, nor is there a Darwin family letter in the archive). Robertson replied to Eggleston with a copy of Lady Hope's account as published in *Baptist World,* but Eggleston did not mention it in his "Charles Darwin's Testimony."

14. "Friends"; Mackenzie, *Booth-Tucker*; Wisbey, *Soldiers,* p. 226; Pebbles, "Commissioner and Mrs. Booth-Tucker"; Booth-Tucker and Booth-Tucker, "Our Tour"; Booth-Tucker, *Six-Six-Six,* p. 9.

15. Coletta, *William Jennings Bryan,* pp. 208–20; Marsden, *Fundamentalism,* pp. 164–75; Numbers, *Creationists,* pp. 41–44.

16. Marsden, *Fundamentalism,* pp. 118–19; Furniss, *Fundamentalist Controversy,* p. 52; Edmondson, "Fundamentalist Sects"; Dozier et al., *Genealogy,* pp. 32–59; "Ex-educator Succumbs."

17. Bryan, *The Bible and Its Enemies,* pp. 44–46; W. Norton to W. J. Bryan, Feb. 7, 1922, William Jennings Bryan Papers, General Correspondence, 35.

18. No doubt confusions, respectively, with Moody's school at Northfield, A. T. Robertson, and the *Watchman-Examiner.*

19. *Harvard University Quinquennial Catalogue*; Ivan Panin, in Evangelical Library; Panin, *Writings.*

20. See Burkhardt and Smith, *Calendar,* nos. 8957, 8962, 9802, 9808, 10194, 10201.

21. Bole, *Confessions;* Numbers, *Creationists,* pp. 55–56, 172; S. J. Bole to

W. J. Bryan, Jan. 9, 1922, William Jennings Bryan Papers, General Correspondence, 35.

22. W. J. Bryan to S. J. Bole, July 27, 1922, S. James Bole Papers. Bryan's other letters in the papers are dated Jan. 16, 1922 and July 2, 1925. The latter invited Bole to Dayton, Tennessee, to assist the prosecution in the Scopes trial.

23. Bole, "Satan's Triangle"; Bole, *Modern Triangle,* pp. 66, 193.

24. Atkins, *Down,* pp. 103–4; E. Darwin to G. Darwin, Jan. 31 and Feb. 8, 1881, Darwin Archive 210.3; also E. Darwin to H. Litchfield, [Jan. 1881?], Darwin Archive 219.2; Sloan, "Demythologizing," p. 109. The hymn "There is a green hill far away" appears in the unabridged edition of Sankey's *Sacred Songs and Solos,* no. 614.

Appendix C
Darwinian Denials

1. Raverat, *Period Piece,* p. 147.
2. J. L. Howe to A. T. Robertson, Dec. 8, 1915, A. T. Robertson Correspondence.
3. Foote, *Infidel Death-beds.*
4. B. Darwin, *World.*
5. See J. A. Derome to A. T. Robertson, Oct. 1, 1930, A. T. Robertson Correspondence, for this additional detail.
6. Keynes, *Leonard Darwin.*
7. B. Barlow, *Family Affair.*

Appendix D
Mr. Fegan Protests

1. A. W. Tiffin to A. Sowerbutts, Mar. 25, 1977; A. W. Tiffin to C. Russell, Nov. 14 and Dec. 6, 1978. The paragraphing of the Kensit letter may have been slightly altered in reconstruction.
2. Not found.
3. Fegan's father died on Jan. 11, 1880, according to the headstone in Downe parish churchyard.

4. In summer 1880 Fegan first held the services. See "Downe, Orpington Kent" and "Notes and Comments."

5. On Darwin's honorary membership and donations to the South American Missionary Society, see Desmond and Moore, *Darwin*, pp. 574–75, 632, 675.

6. Litchfield, *Emma Darwin*, 2:173–75, 244.

7. Cf. App. C.

8. Sir James Hope was sixty-nine and Elizabeth Cotton thirty-five at the time of their marriage.

Appendix E
When Did Lady Hope
Visit Down House?

1. Symons, *British Rainfall*, pp. 56, 60; "Kent in the Hop-picking Season"; J. B. Marsh, *Hops and Hopping*, pp. 42–45.

2. Aveling, *Religious Views*, p. 2; recollections of F. Darwin, Darwin Archive

140.3:79; Desmond and Moore, *Darwin*, pp. 655–57.

3. Cf. Burkhardt and Smith, *Calendar*, nos. 13368, 13371, and 13411 with F. Darwin and Seward, *More Letters*, 2:432 for the October absence.

4. E. Darwin to H. Litchfield, Sept. 13, 1881, Darwin Archive 219.2; "Mr. Fegan and His Work."

5. E. Darwin to H. Litchfield, Oct. 2, 1881, Darwin Archive 219.2.

Appendix F
Darwin's "Other Book"

1. Melton, *Encyclopedia*, 1:470.

2. Royer, "Evolution Yecccccch."

3. Freeman, *Works*, pp. 18–19; Royer, "Evolution: Darwin's 'Other Book.'"

4. Interviews with Chris and Maria Royer, Dec. 11–12, 1980, Salem, West Virginia.

BIBLIOGRAPHY

Manuscripts and Archival Sources

Anglican Cemetery Necropolis, Sydney, New South Wales
Billy Graham Center Library and Archives, Wheaton, Illinois
S. James Bole Papers, Nebraska State Historical Society, Lincoln
Bradlaugh Papers, Bishopsgate Institute, London
William Jennings Bryan Papers, Library of Congress, Washington, D. C.
Chalmers Presbyterian Church Archives, Toronto
Darwin Archive, Cambridge University Library, Cambridge
Darwin Museum, Down House, Downe, Kent
Denny Family Papers, Hingham, Norfolk
Evangelical Library, London
General Register Office, London
Harvard University Archives, Cambridge, Massachusetts
High Court of Justice in Bankruptcy, The Old Bailey, London
Huxley Papers, Imperial College of Science and Technology, London
Kent Archives Office, Maidstone
Metropolitan Toronto Central Library
Moody Papers, Moody Museum, East Northfield, Massachusetts
National Meterological Archives, Bracknell, Berkshire
Northfield Mount Hermon School Archives, Northfield, Massachusetts
Principal Register of Probate, Somerset House, London
Public Record Office, Kew
Registrar-General, Hobart, Tasmania
Registr of Births, Deaths and Marriages, Sydney, New South Wales
A. T. Robertson Correspondence, Southern Baptist Theological Seminary,
  Louisville
Salvation Army Archives and Research Center, New York City
Salvation Army International Heritage Center, London
Scottish Record Office, Edinburgh
Wedgwood-Mosley Collection, Keele University Library, Keele, Staffordshire
YMCA Historical Library, New York City

187

Literature of the Legend

Books and Periodicals

Amos, C. W. Hale. "Darwin's Last Hours." *Reformation Review* (Amsterdam), 4 (Oct. 1956), pp. 56–57.

————. "Darwin's Last Hours." *Monthly Record of the Free Church of Scotland* (Edinburgh), 58 (Feb. 1957), p. 33.

————. "Darwin's Last Hours." *Good Tidings* (St. John's, Newfoundland), 23 (May–June 1967), p. 36.

Anderson, Robert. *In Defence: A Plea for the Faith*. London: Hodder & Stoughton, 1907.

————. *A Doubter's Doubts about Science and Religion; or, In Defence: A Plea for the Faith*. 3d ed. London: Pickering & Inglis, 1924 [1889].

Anon. "Charles Darwin." *A Message from God* (Exeter, Devon), Oct. 1955, pp. 6–8.

Anon. "Darwin on His Death-bed." *Bible Numerics* (Auckland, New Zealand), Nov. 1935, pp. [11–13].

Anon. "Darwin's Last Days." *Christian Fundamentalist* (Minneapolis), 1 (Dec. 1927), p. 12.

Anon. "Darwin's Religious Life." *Bombay Guardian* (Bombay), Mar. 25, 1916, p. 6.

Anon. "Darwin Went Home . . . to The Bible." *National Educator* (Fullerton, Calif.), July 1975, pp. 13, 16.

Anon. *The Evolution Theory Examined*. Chester Springs, Pa.: Layman's Home Missionary Movement, n.d.

Anon. "Magazine Articles." *Bible-Science Newsletter*, Dec. 15, 1969, p. 7.

Anon. "Myths about Darwin." *Literary Guide and Rationalist Review* (London), June 1937, p. 103.

Anon. "News and Notes." *The Tablet* (London), 145 (May 2, 1925), p. 576.

Anon. "Questions and Answers on Creationism." *Bible-Science Newsletter*, Dec. 1986, p. 16.

Anon. "The Untold Story of Charles Darwin." *The Flame* (Southport, Lancs.), Jan.–Feb. 1977, pp. 6–7.

Atkins, Hedley. *Down, the Home of the Darwins: The Story of a House and the People Who Lived There*. Rev. ed. London: Phillimore for the Royal College of Surgeons of England, 1976 [1974].

Barlow, Lady Nora [née Darwin]. "Charles Darwin's 'Conversion'" (letter). *The Scotsman* (Edinburgh), May 8, 1958, p. 6.

Baxter, J. Sidlow. *Awake, My Heart: Daily Devotional and Expository Studies-in-Brief Based on a Variety of Bible Truths, and Covering One Complete Year*. London: Marshall, Morgan & Scott, 1959.

Bole, S. J. *The Battlefield of Faith*. University Park, Iowa: College Press, 1940.

Booth-Tucker, F. "Charles Darwin's Last Days" (letter). *The Christian* (London), Mar. 9, 1922, p. 26.

Bowden, M[alcolm]. "A Return to Faith?" *The Rise of the Evolution Fraud: An Exposure of Its Roots*, pp. 188–93. San Diego, Calif.: Creation-Life Publishers, 1982.

Brown, Frank Burch. *The Evolution of Darwin's Religious Views*. National Association of Baptist Professors of Religion, Special Studies Series, no. 10. Macon, Ga.: Mercer University Press, 1986.

B[urrell], D[avid] J[ames]. "Evolution." *Bible Champion* (Minneapolis), May 1924, pp. 241–44.

Burrowes, W. D. "The Secret of the Sixth Edition of 'The Origin.'" *North American Creation Movement Newsletter*, 32 (1984), pp. 2–3.

[Chadwick, S.] "The Editor's Letter: . . . Darwin on Darwinianism." *Joyful News and Methodist Chronicle* (London), Mar. 8, 1928, p. 3.

Clark, Ronald W. *The Survival of Charles Darwin: A Biography of a Man and an Idea*. London: Weidenfeld & Nicolson, 1984.

Cooper, Thomas. "Charles Darwin; and the Fallacies of Evolution: (A Discourse delivered chiefly to Working Men, in various parts of the Country)." *Thoughts at Fourscore and Earlier: A Medley*, pp. 132–62. London: Hodder & Stoughton, 1885.

Croft, L. R. *The Life and Death of Charles Darwin*. Chorley, Lancs.: Elmwood Books, 1989.

Currey, John Ellis. "The Good Word: Darwin's Beliefs Defended." *Evening Telegram* (St. John's, Newfoundland), Aug. 7, 1993, p. 15a.

Darwin, Leonard. "Myths about Darwin" (letter). *The Times* (London), Aug. 15, 1934, p. 11.

Davidheiser, Bolton. *Evolution and Christian Faith*. Grand Rapids, Mich.: Baker Book House, 1969.

———. "Darwin's Illness." *Science and the Bible*, pp. 89–91. Grand Rapids, Mich: Baker Book House, 1971.

Derome, J. A. "A Weekly Meditation: Was Darwin an Atheist?" *Daily Argus-Leader* (Sioux Falls, S.D.), pt. IX, Oct. 5; pt. X, Oct. 12; pt. XI, Oct. 19, 1930, all p. 6.

Dunkin, F. S. "Darwin's Deathbed" (letter). *Local Preachers' Magazine* (London), 78 (Jan. 1928), pp. 18–19.

E., G. M. "The Evolution Fable" (letter). *Life of Faith* (London), 49 (Jan. 14, 1925), pp. 35–36.

Enoch, H. "Darwin's Recantation." *Evolution or Creation*, pp. 165–67. London: Evangelical Press, 1966.

Fawkes, Leonard. "Darwin's Dying Wish" (letter). *Bromley and Kentish Times* (Bromley, Kent), Nov. 7, 1958, p. 12.

Foote, G. W. "Charles Robert Darwin." *Infidel Death-beds*, pp. 45–46. New ed., rev. by A. D. McLaren. London: Pioneer Press for the Secular Society, [1933].

Freeman, R. B. *The Works of Charles Darwin: An Annotated Bibliographical Handlist.* 2d ed. rev. Folkestone, Kent: Wm Dawson & Sons, 1977 [1965].

———. "Hope, Lady." *Charles Darwin: A Companion*, pp. 165–66. Folkestone, Kent: Dawson, 1978.

Gregory, Maurice. "The Basis of Morals: Final Article—Eugenics and the Superman." *Honour* (London), 7 (June 1917), pp. 39–45.

Hardie, Alexander. *Evolution: Is It Philosophical, Scientific or Scriptural?* Los Angeles: Times-Mirror Press, 1924.

Hawton, Hector. "Personally Speaking: The Myth of Darwin's Conversion." *The Humanist* (London), 73 (July 1958), pp. 4–5.

Hedtke, Randall. *The Secret of the Sixth Edition.* New York: Vantage Press, 1983.

Herbert, David. "Deathbed Repentance: Fabricated or True?" *Darwin's Religious Views: From Creationist to Evolutionist*, pp. 85–93. London, Ont.: Hersil Publications, 1990.

Hope, Lady [Elizabeth Reid Denny, née Cotton]. "Darwin and Christianity." *Watchman-Examiner* (Boston), n.s., 3 (Aug. 19, 1915), p. 1071.

———. "Darwin and Christianity." *Baptist World* (Louisville), 19 (Sept. 9, 1915), p. 11.

Johnston, Alasdair. "Like Darwin, I doubt . . ." (letter). *The Scotsman* (Edinburgh), Apr. 15, 1958, p. 6.

———. "Charles Darwin's 'Conversion'" (letter). *The Scotsman* (Edinburgh), May 8, 1958, p. 6.

Joy, A. F. "'Was Darwin a Christian?'" (letter). *Life of Faith* (London), 49 (Feb. 4, 1925), p. 131.

Le Lievre, A. "'Was Darwin a Christian?'" (letter). *Life of Faith* (London), 49 (Feb. 11, 1925), p. 152.

Litchfield, Henrietta [née Darwin]. "Charles Darwin's Death-bed: Story of Conversion Denied" (letter). *The Christian* (London), Feb. 23, 1922, p. 12.

MacAlister, John. *The Scientific Proof of Origins by Creation.* Midland, Tex.: privately printed, [1983?].

McIver, Tom. "Ancient Tales and Space-Age Myths of Creationist Evangelism." *Skeptical Inquirer,* 10 (Spring 1986), pp. 258–76.

Myers, John, ed. "Lady Hope's Visit with Charles Darwin." *Voices from the Edge of Eternity,* pp. 239–40. Northridge, Calif.: Voice Publications, 1968.

Naismith, A. "Evolutionist—Deathbed of an." *1200 Notes, Quotes, and Anecdotes,* p. 63. London: Pickering & Inglis, 1962.

Newman, Robert C. "The Darwin Conversion Story: An Update." *Creation Research Society Quarterly,* 29 (Sept. 1992), pp. 70–72.

Panin, Ivan. "Darwin on His Deathbed." *Bible Numerics* (Aldershot, Ont.), May–June 1916.

———. [editorial note]. *Bible Numerics* (Aldershot, Ont.), Sept. 1927, pp. 10–11.

———. "Darwin on His Deathbed Again." *Bible Numerics* (Aldershot, Ont.), May–June 1928, pp. 3–31.

———. "Darwin Dies a Christian." *Bible Numerics* (Aldershot, Ont.), Sept.–Oct. 1928, pp. 3–21.

Pastor Mel. "'Learn from the Mistakes of Others and You Won't Live Long Enough to Make Them All Yourself.'" *Faith Seed* (?), [1983?].

Pearce, E. K. Victor. "Darwin, Charles Robert (1809–1882)." In J. D. Douglas, ed., *The New International Dictionary of the Christian Church,* p. 283. Exeter, Devon: Paternoster Press, 1978.

Phippin, Ron. "Return to Faith" (letter). *Radio Times* (London), Jan. 12–19, 1979, p. 71.

Pollock, A. J. "Charles Darwin's Deathbed." *British Evangelist* (London), 47 (Dec. 1920), p. 92.

———. "Charles Darwin's Deathbed." *Churchman's Magazine* (London), 79 (Mar. 1925), p. 69.

Protonius. "Another Darwin Myth." *Literary Guide and Rationalist Review* (London), Oct. 1934, p. 178.

[Royer, Chris W.]. "Evolution Yeccccccch." *Advocate of Truth* (Salem, W. Va.), 19 (Feb. 3, 1969), pp. 2, 9.

[———]. The Editor of "The Advocate of Truth." "Evolution: 'Darwin's Other Book.'" *Truth and Liberty* (Wentworthville, N. S. W.), 18 (May 1970), pp. 14–15.

Rusch, Wilbert H., Sr. "Darwin's Last Hours." *Creation Research Society Quarterly,* 12 (Sept. 1975), pp. 99–102.

———. "Darwin's Last Hours Revisited." *Creation Research Society Quarterly,* 21 (June 1984), pp. 37–39.

———, and Klotz, John W. *Did Charles Darwin Become a Christian?* Ed. Emmett L. Williams. Norcross, Ga.: Creation Research Society Books, 1988.

Sloan, Pat. "The Myth of Darwin's Conversion." *The Humanist* (London), 75 (Mar. 1960), pp. 70–72.

———. "Demythologizing Darwin." *The Humanist* (London), 80 (Apr. 1965), pp. 106–10.

Smith, Oswald J. "Why I Am against Evolution." *The Challenge of Life,* pp. 96–106. London: Marshall, Morgan & Scott, [1946].

———. "The Untold Story of Charles Darwin." *United Holiness Sentinel,* Mar. 1982, pp. 6–7.

[————]. "The Untold Story of Charles Darwin." *Berean Ambassador*, July 1989.

Stone, Irving. "The Death of Darwin." *New Scientist*, Apr. 8, 1982, p. 92.

Taylor, Ian T. *In the Minds of Men: Darwin and the New World Order.* Toronto: TFE Publishing, 1984.

Townsend, L. T. *Collapse of Evolution*, pp. 122–24. Rev. ed. Louisville, Ky.: Pentecostal Publishing Co., [1921].

Turner, C. E. A. "Darwin and Lady Hope." *"Creation": The Journal of the Evolution Protest Movement* (Hounslow, Middx.), 2 (July 1979), p. 4.

T[ilney], A. G. *Darwin and Christianity.* Evolution Protest Movement Pamphlet no. [80]. Hayling Island, Hants.: printed by A. E. Norris & Sons, 1959; new ed., reprinted for the Creation Science Movement, Nov. 1980.

————. *Charles Darwin: The Man.* Evolution Protest Movement Pamphlet no. 176. Hayling Island, Hants.: printed by A. E. Norris & Sons, 1970.

Verey, David, ed. *The Diary of a Victorian Squire: Extracts from the Diaries and Letters of Dearman and Emily Birchall.* Gloucester: Alan Sutton, 1983.

Viator. "Was Darwin a Christian?" (letter). *Life of Faith* (London), 49 (Jan. 28, 1925), p. 93.

Williams, C. F. "Darwin's Deathbed—A Contradiction by His Grandson" (letter). *Local Preachers' Magazine* (London), 78 (Feb. 1928), pp. 43–44.

Tracts

Amos, C. W. Hale. *Darwin's Last Hours.* Phoenix, Ariz.: A. H. Woods, n.d. 4pp.

Anon. *Darwin on His Deathbed.* Lowestoft, Suffolk: printed at Caxton Press, [before 1971]. 4pp.

Anon. *Darwin's Last Hours.* [from Townsend, *Collapse*, 1921; reprinted in Rusch, "Darwin's Last Hours," 1975]

Gauss, J. H. *What Some Scientists Have Said about Evolution.* [St. Louis, Mo.?: Brookes Bible Institute?, before 1925; cited in Joy, "'Was Darwin a Christian?'" 1925]

P[ollock], A. J. *Charles Darwin's Deathbed.* Golden, Colo.: Gospel Publications, n.d. 4pp.

Pratt, [S. J.] *What Is Truth? Was Charles Darwin a Christian? Lady Hope's Testimony.* Lower Sydenham, Kent: printed by Gough, [1925?]. 9pp.

Pringle, Rhodes, ed. *Darwin Returned to the Bible.* Bellingham, Wash.: Faith Mission Publishing, n.d. 4pp.

Rusch, Wilbert H., Sr. *Darwin's Last Hours*. Reprinted from the "Creation Research Society Quarterly," 1975. 8pp.

Smith, Oswald J. *Charles Darwin, "The Believer"*. Randleman, N.C.: Pilgrim Tract Society, n.d. 4pp.

———. *Darwin, "The Believer"*. Independence, Mo.: Gospel Tract Society, n.d. 4pp.; Edmonton, Alta.: Evangelical Tract Distributors, n.d. 4pp.

———, ed. *Darwin's Confession*. Willowdale, Ont.: The People's Church, n.d. 4pp.

———. *The Untold Story of Charles Darwin* [reprinted under the same title in *United Holiness Sentinel*, 1982].

General Literature

Abbott, Lawrence F. *Twelve Great Modernists*. New York: Doubleday, Page, 1927.

"Admiral Sir James Hope." *The Times* (London), June 10, 1881, p. 5.

Ahlstrom, Sydney, and Robert Bruce Mullin. *The Scientific Theist: A Life of Francis Ellingwood Abbot*. Macon, Ga.: Mercer University Press, 1987.

Annual Report of Chalmers' Church for the Year Ending December 31st 1889. Toronto: printed at Mail Job Print, 1890.

Arnstein, Walter Leonard. *The Bradlaugh Case: Atheism, Sex, and Politics among the Late Victorians*. New ed. Columbia: University of Missouri Press, 1983.

Atkins, Hedley. *Down, the Home of the Darwins: The Story of a House and the People Who Lived There*. Rev. ed. London: Phillimore for the Royal College of Surgeons of England, 1976 [1974].

Aveling, Edward B. "A Visit to Charles Darwin." *National Reformer* (London), n.s., 40 (Oct. 22, 1882), pp. 273–74; (Oct. 29, 1882), pp. 291–93.

———. *The Religious Views of Charles Darwin*. London: Freethought Publishing Co., 1883.

Banks, J. A. *Victorian Values: Secularism and the Size of Families*. London: Routledge & Kegan Paul, 1981.

Barlow, Brigit. *A Family Affair*. Lewes, Sussex: Book Guild, 1990.

Barlow, Nora, ed. *The Autobiography of Charles Darwin, 1809–1882, with Original Omissions Restored*. London: Collins, 1958.

Barrett, Paul H.; Peter J. Gautrey; Sandra Herbert; David Kohn; and Sydney Smith, eds. *Charles Darwin's Notebooks, 1836–1844: Geology, Transmutation of Species, Metaphysical Enquiries*. Cambridge: British Museum (Natural History / Cambridge University Press, 1987).

———; Donald J. Weinshank; and Timothy T. Gottleber, eds. *A Concordance to Darwin's "Origin of Species," First Edition.* Ithaca, N.Y.: Cornell University Press, 1981.

Bean, Philip, and Joy Melville. *Lost Children of the Empire.* London: Unwin Hyman, 1989.

Bebbington, D. W. *Evangelicalism in Modern Britain: A History from the 1730s to the 1980s.* London: Unwin Hyman, 1989.

Beer, Gillian. *Darwin's Plots: Evolutionary Narrative in Darwin, George Eliot and Nineteenth-Century Fiction.* London: Routledge & Kegan Paul, 1983.

Bennett, J. H., ed. *Natural Selection, Heredity, and Eugenics; including Selected Correspondence of R. A. Fisher with Leonard Darwin and Others.* Oxford: Clarendon Press, 1983.

"Bible Study Course and Special Addresses at The Northfield Schools and Conferences." *Northfield Schools Bulletin* (East Northfield, Mass.), 3 (Aug. 1915), [pp. 1–4].

Bole, S. J. *Confessions of a College Professor.* Los Angeles, Calif.: Biola Book Room, 1922.

———. "Satan's Triangle: Evolution, Philosophy, Criticism." *The King's Business* (Los Angeles), 16 (May 1925), pp. 199, 231–32; (June 1925), pp. 252–53; (July 1925), pp. 298, 329–30; (Aug. 1925), pp. 348–50; (Sept. 1925), pp. 384–85; (Oct. 1925), pp. 424, 454–55; (Nov. 1925), pp. 475, 514–16; (Dec. 1925), pp. 547, 597–99.

———. *The Modern Triangle: Evolution, Philosophy and Criticism.* Los Angeles, Calif.: Biola Book Room, 1926.

Booth, William. "The Late Mr. T. A. Denny." *War Cry* (London), Jan. 8, 1910, pp. 9–10; Jan. 15, 1910, p. 9; Jan. 22, 1910, pp. 9–10; Jan. 29, 1910, pp. 9–10.

Booth-Tucker, F. *Six-Six-Six: The Mark of the Beast.* London: Marshall Brothers, [c. 1922].

———, and Mrs. Booth-Tucker. "Our Tour in America." *War Cry* (New York), Jan. 14, 1922, pp. 5, 14.

Bradlaugh, Charles, and Annie Besant, eds. *The National Secular Society's Almanack for 1890.* London: Freethought Publishing Co., 1890.

Braithwaite, Robert. *The Life and Letters of Rev. William Pennefather, B. A.* London: Shaw, [1878].

The Bromley Directory. Bromley: Strong, 1880.

Brown, Joyce. "Sir Proby Cautley (1802–1871), a Pioneer of Indian Irrigation." *History of Technology,* 3 (1978), pp. 35–89.

Browne, Janet. "The Charles Darwin—Joseph Hooker Correspondence: An Analysis of Manuscript Resources and Their Use in Biography."

Journal of the Society for the Bibliography of Natural History, 8 (1978), pp. 351–66.

Bryan, William Jennings. *The Bible and Its Enemies.* New ed. Chicago: Bible Institute Colportage Association, 1921.

Burkhardt, Frederick, and Sydney Smith, eds. *A Calendar of the Correspondence of Charles Darwin, 1821–1882.* New York: Garland, 1985.

———, eds. *The Correspondence of Charles Darwin, 1821–1882.* 9 vols. to date. Cambridge: Cambridge University Press, 1985–94.

Carter, Burnham. *So Much to Learn: The History of the Northfield Mount Hermon School in Commemoration of the 100th Anniversary, 1980.* Northfield, Mass.: Northfield Mount Hermon School, 1976.

"Charles Darwin on Religion." *National Reformer* (London), n.s., 40 (Oct. 22, 1882), p. 273.

Clark, Ronald W. *The Life of Bertrand Russell.* Harmondsworth, Middx.: Penguin Books, 1978.

Clinch, George. *English Hops: A History of Cultivation and Preparation for the Market from the Earliest Times.* London: McCorquodale, [1919].

Coad, F. Roy. *A History of the Brethren Movement: Its Origins, Its Worldwide Development, and Its Significance for the Present Day.* Exeter, Devon: Paternoster Press, 1968.

Coletta, Paolo E. *William Jennings Bryan: III. Political Puritan, 1915–1925.* Lincoln: University of Nebraska Press, 1969.

College Y.M.C.A. Souvenir: Summer School for Bible Study, Mt. Hermon, Mass., July, 1886. [Mt. Hermon, Mass.: privately printed, 1886].

Colp, Ralph, Jr. "The Contacts of Charles Darwin with Edward Aveling and Karl Marx." *Annals of Science,* 33 (1976), pp. 387–94.

———. *To Be an Invalid: The Illness of Charles Darwin.* Chicago: University of Chicago Press, 1977.

———. "Charles Darwin's Coffin and Its Maker." *Journal of the History of Medicine and Allied Sciences,* 35 (1980), pp. 59–63.

———. "Charles Darwin's Reprobation of Nature: 'Clumsy, Wasteful, Blundering Low & Horribly Cruel.'" *New York State Journal of Medicine,* 81 (1981), pp. 1116–19.

———. "The Myth of the Darwin–Marx Letter." *History of Political Economy,* 14 (1982), pp. 461–82.

———. "Charles Darwin's Dream of His Double Execution." *Journal of Psychohistory,* 13 (1986), pp. 277–92.

———. "'Confessing a Murder': Darwin's First Revelations about Transmutation." *Isis,* 77 (1986), pp. 9–32.

———. "Charles Darwin's 'insufferable grief.'" *Free Associations,* no. 9 (1987), pp. 7–44.

Coxe, Antony D. Hippisley. *Haunted Britain: A Guide to Supernatural Sites Frequented by Ghosts, Witches, Poltergeists and Other Mysterious Beings.* London: Hutchinson, 1973.

Darwin, Bernard. *The World That Fred Made: An Autobiography.* London: Chatto & Windus, 1955.

Darwin, Charles. *On the Origin of Species by Means of Natural Selection, or the Preservation of Favoured Races in the Struggle for Life.* London: John Murray, 1859.

———. *The Descent of Man and Selection in Relation to Sex.* 2d ed. London: John Murray, 1874.

———, and Alfred Russel Wallace. *Evolution by Natural Selection.* Ed. Gavin de Beer. Cambridge: at the University Press, 1958.

Darwin, Francis, ed. *The Life and Letters of Charles Darwin, including an Autobiographical Chapter.* 3 vols. London: John Murray, 1887.

———, and A. C. Seward, eds. *More Letters of Charles Darwin: A Record of His Work in a Series of Hitherto Unpublished Letters.* 2 vols. London: John Murray, 1903.

Darwin, Leonard. *What Is Eugenics?* London: Watts, 1928.

———. "Memories of Down House." *Nineteenth Century,* 106 (July 1929), pp. 118–23.

Dawson, Oswald. *An Indictment of Darwin.* London: Freethought Publishing Co., 1888.

Death's Test; or, Christian Lies about Dying Infidels. London: Freethought Publishing Co., 1882.

"Defend Orthodoxy: No Doubts at Northfield . . ." *Springfield Daily Republican* (Springfield, Mass.), Aug. 4, 1915, p. 4.

Desmond, Adrian. "Robert E. Grant: The Social Predicament of a Pre-Darwinian Transmutationist." *Journal of the History of Biology,* 17 (1984), pp. 189–223.

———. *The Politics of Evolution: Morphology, Medicine, and Reform in Radical London.* Chicago: University of Chicago Press, 1989.

———, and James Moore. *Darwin,* London: Michael Joseph, 1991,

Dingle, A. E. *The Campaign for Prohibition in Victorian England.* London: Croom Helm, 1980.

"Down, Orpington, Kent." *The Christian* (London), Mar. 24, 1881, p. 16.

[Dozier, Melville et al.] *Genealogy and Life Sketches of the Dozier Brothers.* [Shanghai? privately printed, 1936?].

Dreyer, Peter. *A Gardener Touched with Genius: The Life of Luther Burbank.* New York: Coward, McCann, & Geoghegan, 1975.

Edmondson, William D. "Fundamentalist Sects of Los Angeles, 1900–1930." Ph.D. diss., Claremont Graduate School, 1969.

Eggleston, J. D. "Charles Darwin's Testimony to Christian Missionaries." *Moody Bible Institute Monthly* (Chicago), 30 (Mar. 1930), pp. 332–33.

Erskine, Fiona. "Darwin in Context: The London Years, 1837–1842." Ph.D. thesis, Open University, 1987.

"Ex-Educator Succumbs: Melville Dozier dies of age infirmities; served in Civil War." *Los Angeles Times*, Oct. 18, 1936, pt. 2, pp. 1–2.

Extraordinary Tithe Charge: Parishes in the Counties of Kent and Sussex in which an Extraordinary Tithe Charge for Hops, Market Gardens, and Orchard or Fruit Plantations was distinguished at the time of Commutation, with the Acreage then under such Cultivation respectively, and the Amount of Extraordinary Charge per Acre, and also the Acreage under such Cultivation in the Year 1880, showing for each Parish the Total Area and Population, the Total Amount of Tithe, Rent-Charge and Extraordinary Tithe levied in the Year 1880, and the Appropriation of the same respectively. Parliamentary Papers, 1882, vol. 50. London: Henry Hansard, 1882.

Fegan, J. W. C. "A Personal Tribute to Sir R. Anderson." *The Christian* (London), Nov. 28, 1918, p. 20.

"Fifty Years of Progress." Chalmers Presbyterian Church, 1877–1927: Anniversary Services. [Toronto: privately printed, 1927].

Findlay, James F., Jr. *Dwight L. Moody, American Evangelist, 1837–1899.* Chicago: University of Chicago Press, 1969.

Foote, G. W. *Darwin on God.* London: Progressive Publishing Co., 1889.

———. *Infidel Death-beds.* New ed., rev. by A. D. McLaren. London: Pioneer Press for the Secular Society, [1933].

Freeman, R. B. *The Works of Charles Darwin: An Annotated Bibliographical Handlist.* 2d ed. rev. Folkestone, Kent: Wm Dawson & Sons, 1977 [1965].

"Friends of the Army.—XLII. T. A. Denny, Esq." *All the World* (London), June 1909, pp. 291–94.

Fullerton, W. Y. *J. W. C. Fegan: A Tribute.* London: Marshall, Morgan & Scott, [1930].

Furniss, Norman F. *The Fundamentalist Controversy, 1918–1931.* New Haven, Conn.: Yale University Press, 1954.

Gay, Peter. *The Bourgeois Experience: Victoria to Freud,* vol. 1, *The Education of the Senses.* New York: Oxford University Press, 1984.

Gill, Everett. *A. T. Robertson: A Biography.* New York: Macmillan, 1943.

Harvard University Quinquennial Catalogue of the Officers and Graduates, 1636–1925. Cambridge, Mass.: published by the University, 1925.

Haeckel, Ernst. *Die Naturanschauung von Darwin, Goethe und Lamarck: Vortrag in der ersten öffentlichen Sitzung der fünfundfünfzigsten Ver-*

sammlung Deutscher Naturforscher und Aerzte zu Eisenach am 18. September 1882. Jena: Gustav Fischer, 1882.

———. "Professor Haeckel on Darwin, Goethe, and Lamarck." *Nature,* 26 (Sept. 28, 1882), pp. 533–41.

Hammerton, A. James. *Emigrant Gentlewomen: Genteel Poverty and Female Emigration, 1830–1914.* London: Croom Helm, 1979.

Harvey, David. "Fruit Growing in Kent in the Nineteenth Century." In Margaret Roake and John Whyman, eds., *Essays in Kentish History,* pp. 213–26. London: Frank Cass, 1973.

Heasman, Kathleen. *Evangelicals in Action: An Appraisal of Their Social Work in the Victorian Era.* London: Bles, 1962.

"A Hitherto Unpublished Letter of Charles Darwin." *National Reformer* (London), n.s., 40 (Oct. 1, 1882), p. 235.

Hope, Lady [i.e., Elizabeth Reid Cotton]. *Our Coffee-Room.* 6th ed. London: Nisbet, 1877.

——— [i.e., Elizabeth Reid Cotton]. *More about Our Coffee-Room.* London: Nisbet, 1878.

———. *Lines of Light on a Dark Background.* London: Nisbet, 1879.

———. "Coffee-Rooms for the People." *Good Words* (London), 21 (Oct. 1880), pp. 749–52; (Dec. 1880), pp. 844–47.

———. "Trained Nursing in Workhouse Infirmaries." *Good Words* (London), 22 (May 1881), pp. 351–54.

———. *Our Golden Key: A Narrative of Facts from "Outcast London."* London: Seeley, Jackson, 1884.

———. "What Shall We Do for the People?" *The Christian* (London), June 10, 1886, p. 8; June 17, 1886, p. 5; July 1, 1886, p. 2; July 15, 1886, p. 3.

———. *General Sir Arthur Cotton, R. E., K. C. S. I.: His Life and Work.* London: Hodder & Stoughton, 1900.

———. "Lady Hope's Appeal." *Daily Mail* (London), May 23, 1907, p. 6.

———. *English Homes and Villages—Kent and Sussex.* Sevenoaks, Kent: Salmon, 1909.

———. "Halls of Happiness." *Watchman-Examiner* (Boston), n.s., 3 (Oct. 21, 1915), p. 1356.

"Hope, Sir James (1808–1881)." *Dictionary of National Biography,* 9:1214.

"Hop-picking." *The Times* (London), Sept. 27, 1881, p. 6.

Howarth, O. J. R. and Eleanor K. *A History of Darwin's Parish, Downe, Kent.* Southampton: Russell, [1933].

Huxley, Leonard. "Huxley's Attitude to Religion" (letter). *Daily Mail* (London), Oct. 3, 1907, p. 6.

———. *Charles Darwin.* London: Watts, 1921.

———. "The Home Life of Charles Darwin." *The R.P.A. Annual for 1921*, pp. 3–9. London: Watts, 1921.

Ivan Panin, 1855–1942. [printed in Canada, n.d.].

Keith, Arthur. "Neglected Darwin." *The R.P.A. Annual for 1923*, pp. 3–9. London: Watts, 1923.

———. *The Religion of a Darwinist*. London: Watts, 1925.

———. *Concerning Man's Origin: Being the Presidential Address Given at the Meeting of the British Association Held in Leeds on August 31, 1927, and Recent Essays on Darwinian Subjects*. London: Watts, 1927.

———. *Darwinism and What It Implies*. London: Watts, 1928.

———. "Darwin Remembered." *The R.P.A. Annual for the Year 1930*, pp. 19–25. London: Watts, 1930.

———. *An Autobiography*. London: Watts, 1950.

———. "Some Anthropological Notes on Darwin and on Members of His Family." *Man*, Dec. 1952, pp. 181–82.

———. *Darwin Revalued*. London: Watts, 1955.

Kent, William. *London for Heretics*. London: Watts, 1932.

"Kent in the Hop-picking Season." *The Times* (London), Sept. 23, 1881, p. 11; Sept. 26, 1881, p. 8; Sept. 29, 1881, p. 8.

Keynes, Margaret. *Leonard Darwin, 1850–1943*. Cambridge: privately printed at Cambridge University Press, 1943.

Kinnaird, Emily. *Reminiscences*. London: John Murray, 1925.

Kohn, David. "Darwin's Ambiguity: The Secularization of Biological Meaning." *British Journal for the History of Science*, 22 (1989), pp. 215–39.

"Lady Hope." *The Christian* (London), Mar. 23, 1922, p. 11.

"Lady Hope Praises Glories of Newport." *New York Times*, July 28, 1914, p. 7.

"The Late Mr. T. A. Denny." *The Christian* (London), Jan. 6, 1910, p. 22.

L[aws], C[urtis] L[ee]. "The Northfield Conference." *Watchman-Examiner* (Boston), n.s., 3 (Aug. 19, 1915), pp. 1067–71.

———. "Summer Days at Northfield." *Watchman-Examiner* (Boston), n.s., 5 (Aug. 30, 1917), pp. 1113–17.

———. "Convention Side Lights." *Watchman-Examiner* (Boston), n.s., 8 (July 1, 1920), pp. 834–35.

"Lawyer, Author, Evangelist: The Late Sir Robert Anderson, K.C.B., LL.D." *The Christian* (London), Nov. 28, 1918, pp. 19–20.

Lewins, Robert. "Mr. Darwin and Professor Haeckel." *Journal of Science*, 3d ser., 4 (Dec. 1882), pp. 751–52.

Lewis, Henry. *Modern Rationalism as Seen at Work in Its Biographies*. London: SPCK, 1913.

"'A Life for Souls.' Mr. J. W. C. Fegan: Evangelist and Philanthropist."
    The Christian (London), Dec. 17, 1925, pp. 25–26.
Lightman, Bernard. "Ideology, Evolution and Late-Victorian Agnostic
    Popularizers." In James R. Moore, ed., *History, Humanity and Evolu-
    tion: Essays for John C. Greene*, pp. 285–309. New York: Cambridge
    University Press, 1989.
Litchfield, Henrietta Emma [née Darwin]. *Richard Buckley Litchfield: A
    Memoir Written for His Friends*. Cambridge: at the University Press,
    1910.
———. *Emma Darwin: A Century of Family Letters, 1792–1896.* 2 vols.
    London: John Murray, 1915 (otherwise 1904 ed., privately printed at
    Cambridge University Press).
Mabie, Janet. *The Years Beyond: The Story of Northfield, D. L. Moody,
    and The Schools*. East Northfield, Mass.: Northfield Bookstore, 1960.
McCalman, I. D. "Popular Irreligion in Early Victorian England: Infidel
    Preachers and Radical Theatricality in 1830s London." In R. W. Davis
    and R. J. Helmstadter, eds., *Religion and Irreligion in Victorian Soci-
    ety: Essays in Honor of R. K. Webb*, pp. 51–67. London: Routledge,
    1992.
McIver, Tom. *Anti-Evolution: An Annotated Bibliography*. Jefferson,
    N.C.: McFarland, 1988.
Mackenzie, F. A. *Booth-Tucker: Sadhu and Saint*. London: Hodder &
    Stoughton, 1930.
M[ackinnon], J[ane]. *Recollections of D. L. Moody and His Work in
    Britain, 1874–1892*. Edinburgh: printed for private circulation, 1905.
McKnight, Edgar V. "A. T. Robertson's Contribution to the Interpreta-
    tion of the New Testament." Th.D. diss., Southern Baptist Theological
    Seminary (Louisville), 1960.
Malmgreen, Gail, ed. *Religion in the Lives of English Women,
    1760–1930*. London: Croom Helm, 1986.
Mandelbaum, Maurice. "Darwin's Religious Views." *Journal of the His-
    tory of Ideas*, 19 (1958), pp. 363–78.
Manier, Edward. *The Young Darwin and His Cultural Circle: A Study
    of the Influences Which Helped Shape the Language and the Logic of
    the First Drafts of the Theory of Natural Selection*. Dordrecht, Hol-
    land: Reidel, 1978.
Mann, W. *Science and the Soul, with a Chapter on Infidel Death-Beds*.
    London: Pioneer Press, 1919.
Marsden, George M. *Fundamentalism in American Culture: The Shap-
    ing of Twentieth-Century Evangelicalism*. New York: Oxford Univer-
    sity Press, 1980.

Marsh, Joan. "Charles Darwin—Justice of the Peace in Bromley, Kent." *Justice of the Peace*, 147 (1983), pp. 636–37.

Marsh, John B. *Hops and Hopping.* London: Simpkin, Marshall, Hamilton, Kent, 1892.

Mayr, Ernst. *One Long Argument: Charles Darwin and the Genesis of Evolutionary Biology.* London: Allen Lane / The Penguin Press, 1991.

Melton, J. Gordon. *The Encyclopedia of American Religions.* 2 vols. Wilmington, N.C.: McGrath Publishing Co., 1978.

"Mr. Fegan and His Work." *The Christian* (London), Oct. 6, 1881, p. 18.

"Mr. T. Anthony Denny." *The Times* (London), Dec. 29, 1909, p. 9.

Montgomery, Hugh Edmund Langton. "Emma Darwin." *The Month*, 29 (1963), pp. 288–94.

Moore, James R. "On the Education of Darwin's Sons: The Correspondence between Charles Darwin and the Reverend G. V. Reed, 1857–1864." *Notes and Records of the Royal Society of London*, 32 (1977), pp. 41–70.

———. *The Post-Darwinian Controversies: A Study of the Protestant Struggle to Come to Terms with Darwin in Great Britain and America, 1870–1900.* Cambridge: Cambridge University Press, 1979.

———. "Charles Darwin Lies in Westminster Abbey." *Biological Journal of the Linnean Society*, 17 (1982), pp. 97–113.

———. "1859 and All That: Remaking the Story of Evolution-and-Religion." In R. G. Chapman and C. T. Duval, eds., *Charles Darwin, 1809–1882: A Centennial Commemorative*, pp. 167–94. Wellington, New Zealand: Nova Pacifica, 1982.

———. "Darwin of Down: The Evolutionist as Squarson-Naturalist." In David Kohn, ed., *The Darwinian Heritage*, pp. 435–81. Princeton, N.J.: Princeton University Press, 1985.

———. "Herbert Spencer's Henchmen: The Evolution of Protestant Liberals in Late Nineteenth-Century America." In John R. Durant, ed., *Darwinism and Divinity: Essays on Evolution and Religious Belief*, pp. 76–100. Oxford: Blackwell, 1985.

———. "Freethought, Secularism, Agnosticism: The Case of Charles Darwin." In Gerald Parsons, ed., *Religion in Victorian Britain*, vol. 1, *Traditions*, pp. 274–319. Manchester: Manchester University Press, 1988.

———, ed. *Religion in Victorian Britain*, vol. 3, *Sources*. Manchester: Manchester University Press, 1988.

———. "Of Love and Death: Why Darwin 'gave up Christianity.'" In James R. Moore, ed., *History, Humanity and Evolution: Essays for John C. Greene*, pp. 195–229. New York: Cambridge University Press, 1989.

Moore-Anderson, A. P. *Sir Robert Anderson, K.C.B., LL.D.: A Tribute and Memoir.* London: Morgan & Scott, 1919.
———. *Sir Robert Anderson, K.C.B., LL.D., and Lady Agnes Anderson.* London: Marshall, Morgan & Scott, 1947.
Mott, Frank Luther. *A History of American Magazines, 1741–1850.* Cambridge, Mass.: Belknap Press of Harvard University Press, 1957.
Mutch, James Robert. *Genealogy of the Mutch Family.* Charlottestown, P. E. I.: printed by Patriot Job Print, 1929.
Mutch, John. "Hosea's Conception of God's Feelings towards Israel: What, How Attained, and How It Influenced All His Teaching." *Knox College Monthly and Presbyterian Magazine* (Toronto), 18 (1894–95), pp. 122–30.
"New Coffee Tavern and Mission at Beckenham." *Bromley Record and Monthly Advertiser* (Bromley, Kent), Mar. 1, 1881, p. 25.
"Notes and Comments." *The Christian* (London), May 19, 1881, p. 16.
Numbers, Ronald L. *The Creationists.* New York: Alfred A. Knopf, 1992.
"Old Beckenham Mission." *Beckenham Journal, and Penge and Sydenham Advertiser*, Mar. 1881, p. 10.
"The Outlook—The Opening of the Church Congress." *Daily Mail* (London), Oct. 1, 1907, p. 6.
Panin, Ivan. *The Writings of Ivan Panin.* New Haven, Conn.: printed for the author by Wilson H. Lee Co., 1918.
Parr, Joy. *Labouring Children: British Immigrant Apprentices to Canada, 1869–1924.* London: Croom Helm, 1980.
Pebbles, Ashley B. "Commissioner and Mrs. Booth-Tucker." *War Cry* (New York), Nov. 26, 1921, pp. 9, 13.
Peckham, Morse, ed. *The Origin of Species by Charles Darwin: A Variorum Text.* Philadelphia: University of Pennsylvania Press, 1959.
Pike, Royston. "Darwin of Downe." *The Humanist*, 73 (July 1958), pp. 16–19.
"Praises English Queens." *New York Times*, Dec. 15, 1913, p. 6.
Prochaska, F. K. *Women and Philanthropy in Nineteenth-Century England.* London: Oxford University Press, 1980.
Proctor, Henry. *Evolution and Regeneration.* London: L. N. Fowler, 1911.
"The Rationalist Press Association Annual Dinner and Reunion." *Literary Guide and Rationalist Review*, July 1931, pp. 119–25.
Raverat, Gwen. *Period Piece: A Cambridge Childhood.* London: Faber & Faber, 1952.
Register of University of Toronto for the Year 1920. Toronto: University of Toronto Press, [1920].
Report from the Select Committee on the Hop Industry; together with the Proceedings of the Committee, Minutes of Evidence, and Appen-

dix. Parliamentary Papers, 1890, vol. 13. London: Henry Hansard, 1890.

"Rev. John Mutch, M. A." *The Westminster* (Toronto), 2 (Apr. 1897), p. 181.

Robertson, A. T. "Darwinism and the South." *Wake Forest Student* (Wake Forest, N.C.), 4 (Jan. 1885), pp. 205–6.

———. "Evolution and Modern Science." *Seminary Magazine* (Louisville, Ky.), 4 (Feb. 1891), pp. 35–36.

———. "The Glory of Jesus: Hebrews I–VIII." *Record of Christian Work* (East Northfield, Mass.), 34 (July 1915), p. 403.

———. "The Prohibition Movement in the South." *Watchman-Examiner* (Boston), n.s., 3 (Dec. 2, 1915), p. 1548.

———. "Scientists and the Future Life." *Christian Index* (Atlanta), Mar. 11, 1926, p. 7.

Robertson, J. Ross. *Landmarks of Toronto: A Collection of Historical Sketches of the Old Town of York from 1792 until 1837 and of Toronto from 1834 to 1904.* Vol. 4. Toronto: Robertson, 1904.

Royle, Edward. *Victorian Infidels: The Origins of the British Secularist Movement, 1791–1866.* Manchester: Manchester University Press, 1974.

———. *Radicals, Secularists and Republicans: Popular Freethought in Britain, 1866–1915.* Manchester: Manchester University Press, 1980.

Rudwick, Martin. "Charles Darwin in London: The Integration of Public and Private Science." *Isis,* 73 (1982), pp. 186–206.

Russell, A. J. *Their Religion.* London: Hodder & Stoughton, 1934.

Sankey, Ira D., ed. *Sacred Songs and Solos: with Standard Hymns, Combined. 750 Pieces.* London: Morgan & Scott, n.d.

Scroggie, W. Graham, ed. *The Story of a Life in the Love of God: Incidents Collected from the Diaries of Mrs. James J. Scroggie.* London: Pickering & Inglis, n.d.

Secord, James. "The Discovery of a Vocation: Darwin's Early Geology." *British Journal for the History of Science,* 24 (1991), pp. 133–57.

Shiman, Lilian Lewis. "The Band of Hope Movement: Respectable Recreation for Working-Class Children." *Victorian Studies,* 17 (1973), pp. 49–74.

———. *Crusade against Drink in Victorian England.* London: Macmillan, 1986.

Smith, F. B. "The Atheist Mission, 1840–1900." In Robert Robson, ed., *Ideas and Institutions of Victorian Britain: Essays in Honour of George Kitson Clark,* pp. 204–35. London: G. Bell, 1967.

Smithers, David Waldron. "Charles Darwin's Wandering Coffin." *Bygone Kent,* 10 (1989), 129–33.

Spencer, Frank. *Piltdown: A Scientific Forgery.* London: Oxford University Press, 1990.

Spivey, Colin. "James Fegan." *Christian Graduate,* June 1970, pp. 33–36.

Stecher, Robert M. "The Darwin–Innes Letters: The Correspondence of an Evolutionist with His Vicar, 1848–1884." *Annals of Science,* 17 (1961), pp. 201–58.

Stratton, J. Y. *Hops and Hop-pickers.* London: SPCK, 1883.

"Sugar Plums." *The Freethinker* (London), 2 (May 7, 1882), p. 149.

Sulloway, Frank J. "Darwin's Conversion: The 'Beagle' Voyage and Its Aftermath." *Journal of the History of Biology,* 15 (1982), pp. 325–96.

Symons, G. J. *British Rainfall, 1881: On the Distribution of Rain over the British Isles during the Year 1881 as Observed at More Than 2000 Stations. . . .* London: Edward Stanford, 1882.

Tatlow, Tissington. *The Story of the Student Christian Movement of Great Britain and Ireland.* London: SCM Press, 1933.

"Tent Services at Bromley." *The Christian* (London), Sept. 2, 1880, p. 5.

Thompson, Vera. "Medical and Social Work." In *Old Days in the Kent Hop Gardens,* pp. 42–52. Tonbridge, Kent: printed by Tonbridge Free Press for the West Kent Women's Institute News, 1962.

Thomson, Keith Stewart, and Stan P. Rachootin. "Turning Points in Darwin's Life." *Biological Journal of the Linnean Society,* 17 (1982), pp. 23–37.

Tribe, David. *President Charles Bradlaugh, M. P.* London: Elek Books, 1971.

Vignoles, O. J. "The Home of a Naturalist." *Good Words* (London), 34 (1893), pp. 95–101.

Wallace, Alfred Russel. *My Life: A Record of Events and Opinions.* 2 vols. London: Chapman & Hall, 1905.

Wedgwood, Barbara and Hensleigh. *The Wedgwood Circle: Four Generations of a Family and Their Friends.* Westfield, N.J.: Eastview Editions, 1980.

Whitehead, Charles. *Hops: From Set to the Sky-Lights.* London: Effingham Wilson, 1881.

———. *Hop Cultivation.* London: John Murray, 1893.

Whyte, A. Gowans. *The Story of the R.P.A., 1899–1949.* London: Watts, 1949.

". . . A Widow's Affairs . . ." *The Times* (London), Apr. 13, 1911, p. 3; June 29, 1911, p. 4; July 20, 1911, p. 3; May 9, 1912, p. 3.

Winks, Robin W., ed. *The Historian as Detective: Essays on Evidence.* New York: Harper & Row, 1969.

Wisbey, Herbert A., Jr. *Soldiers without Swords: A History of the Salvation Army in the United States.* New York: Macmillan, 1956.

INDEX

205

218